THE CLASSICAL BUILDINGS OF BATH

THE CLASSICAL BUILDINGS OF BATH

MIKE JENNER

 redcliffe

Ralph Allen's townhouse. John Wood, 1727.

The publishers thank Knight Frank LLP for their generous financial contribution towards the cost of this publication, which enables it to be published at an accessible price.

First published in 2013 by Redcliffe Press Ltd.
81g Pembroke Road, Bristol BS8 3EA

www.redcliffepress.co.uk
info@redcliffepress.co.uk

ISBN 978-1-908326-03-4

British Library Cataloguing-in-Publication Data
A catalogue record for this book is available from the British Library

Set in Hoefler 11/15
Design and layout Stephen Morris www.stephen-morris.co.uk
Printed in the Czech Republic via Akcent Media

CONTENTS

THE CLASSICAL BUILDINGS OF BATH

Introduction

In the 1970s a woman living in the Royal Crescent painted her front door yellow, despite the long tradition that all external joinery in the great terraces should be painted white, and in contravention of a City Council ruling making it obligatory. When instructed by the Council to change it, she refused. After a long fight she eventually went to the High Court which ruled in her favour. She became a national hero, the little woman standing against over-weening authority. She was right, there must be limits to the power of authority, but she was wrong nonetheless. Bath is the classic example of a community which has accepted such personal restraints for the benefit of everybody. In rejecting them she was guilty of bad manners. If you choose to live in a community it is surely reasonable that you should respect the rules and conventions which have made it a desirable place to live.

In writing this book I have tried to convey an appreciation, and understanding, of the classical street-building tradition as exemplified in Bath, where, more than in any other British city, it reached its purest expression. I am one of the last generation of architects who were trained to draw the elements of classical architecture, and although I knew I was unlikely to use them in my work, I learnt to love them.

So I write as a lover, but I do see the warts. Architectural histories can give the impression that the architects of earlier centuries were all paragons who could do no wrong, and it is only twentieth-century ones who produced ugly buildings. Both those assumptions are nonsense. The younger John Wood, son of the great John Wood, made mistake after mistake; John Eveleigh was an architectural lout; and John Pinch very nearly ruined Queen Square (although traffic has completed the job so efficiently that we no longer notice his damage).

I think part of the explanation of these misconceptions is an insufficient appreciation of fashion. Fashion is like a pendulum, every generation dislikes and reacts against the work of the previous one, and re-appreciates the work of the one before that which their fathers condemned, and so on, ad infinitum. When I was a student at the end of the 1940s it was almost universally believed that good design ended when Queen Victoria ascended the throne. Today the architecture of her years is revered, as is the architecture of the Regency which her subjects condemned. Their loathing extended to the buildings of Robert Adam, he reacted against the work of John Wood's generation and they despised the work of Wren and his school. Today it is almost universally believed that good design ended when Elizabeth II ascended the throne, though the reaction against that is already under way; a few of the London tower blocks have now been Listed. One of the themes of this book is to show how the pendulum of fashion influenced the development of architecture in Bath.

Another theme arises from the fact that a lifetime of architectural practice occasionally lets me understand, almost instinctively, the financial reason why an architect chose the solution he did. In chapter four I record several instances of the great John Wood's cleverness in saving expense in ways that few ever notice, whilst lavishing expenditure in ways that have given pleasure to millions. The most notable example is his invention of the crescent-shaped terrace of houses. He had several reasons for doing that but, I have no doubt whatever, the most compelling one was to save money by building his houses along the contours of the shallow valley instead of crossing them. It is hard to believe now, but nobody, anywhere, had thought of doing that before. His innovation has been imitated across the world ever since. He was a titan.

There is much more to enjoy in Bath than I have been able to mention: the Gothic churches and schools which are outside my classical remit; several terraces which are quite as worthy of attention as some which I have selected; rows of humble cottages which have fronts with classical proportions because their builders had absorbed them from childhood; the wide pavements of Pennant slabs, with their slight variations of colour, which were brought up-river from Bristol where they were quarried; the street names cut with beautiful Roman lettering into walls of houses; the occasional mounting blocks built for gentlemen who could no longer vault into the saddle. The riches of Bath are inexhaustible.

It is hard to write about classical buildings without using technical terms which the general reader cannot be expected to know. I therefore include a short glossary at the end of this book.

Some owners of houses in Bath refused me entry because they feared that publicity would alert burglars to the possessions in their houses, and a considerable number neglected to reply to my letter asking for permission to visit. That is why there are so few photographs of house interiors.

I am much indebted to the staff of Bath Reference Library, the Bath and North East Somerset Record Office, the Somerset Record Office at Taunton, the Roman Baths Museum and the Bath Preservation Trust. The photographer Stephen Morris and I are grateful to the following individuals and institutions who helped us in various ways: Julie Barr, Prof. David Blake, Daniel Brown, Ian Burns, David Crouch, Vera Forsyth, Hilwood Resorts and Hotels Ltd., Steve Johnston, Sally Johnston at Kingswood School, Sharon Love, Jill Mead, Dee Miller, Felix Moore, Mr and Mrs Moss, Gladys Powney, Prior Park College, Kate Rogers, the Royal Crescent Hotel and Morag Scott-Farrer.

Finally, I want to record my appreciation of Stephen Morris's photographs. They greatly enrich this book. Few architectural historians have been so lucky.

Mike Jenner, March 2013.

1 Bath and the ravages of time

Despite what is often said to the contrary, Bath looks more beautiful today than it has done for at least 150 years. That it does so is little short of a miracle. All buildings suffer from the ravages of time – wind, rain, fire, bombardment, vandalism, changes of fashion, and the introduction of new technologies and social arrangements. Bath has suffered from all of those. Many of its already famous buildings were spoilt only a few years after they were built. Pulteney Bridge, for example, was savagely mutilated 20 years after its completion. By the middle of the nineteenth century the city's golden stone was becoming black with soot from the domestic coal fires, and saturated with corrosive acid from its industry and that of upwind Bristol. After a period when Bath was supreme among the British spas, the one place outside London that everybody who was anybody had to visit, it became instead the place to which colonial civil servants retired and their grandchildren were sent to school. The sedan chair, with its delicious aura of intrigue and coquetry, was replaced by the Bath chair, with its dismal aura of invalidism and decline. Bath slept, and nothing disturbed its dreams until the bombing of 1942. Then in a couple of nights, 400 people were killed and 1,061 houses destroyed or so badly damaged that they had to be demolished. Altogether 1900 premises were affected.

By then the city had reached its nadir, where it remained throughout the rest of the war and the following years of austerity. Even before that, throughout the depressed 1920s and 1930s many of its buildings were already showing obvious signs of neglected maintenance, and in the 1950s all of them displayed the additional enforced neglect of six years of war and five of subsequent austerity. Paintwork was cracked and peeling, stone ornaments and balustrades were crumbling. Many of the houses had been cheaply converted into flats and were festooned with pipework from the bathrooms clipped onto their backs, and from the kitchenettes ruining the proportions and plasterwork of the rooms into which they had been uncaringly squeezed. High explosive bombs had ripped holes into world-famous terraces, and incendiary bombs had gutted rows of houses which stood blind and forlorn. The Assembly Rooms were roofless and tottering, the great lawn in front of the Royal Crescent had been turned into allotments, and the railings around the gardens in the squares had been taken to make guns and tanks. The population had grown old, with a high proportion of retired people, many of them eking out inadequate pensions in flats and bedsits. To a young architectural student in 1950 sketching Bath's famously beautiful buildings, the decaying soot-black city was profoundly depressing. Old ladies were eager to show their enchanting fireplaces and plasterwork, but their worn carpets and curtains, in house after house, smelt of stale cooking and urine.

In the 1950s everybody respected and enjoyed the famous terraces and squares, but in the city centre and on the lower slopes there were acres of terraces of tiny artisan houses, and scarcely anybody enjoyed them. They had none of the graces of the grander houses, had grossly inadequate sanitary arrangements and were increasingly tumbledown. The word 'gentrification' was far in the future. It seemed logical and humane to demolish them and re-house their occupants in modern flats. It was only in the mid-sixties that a few people began to realise that these terraces had contextual and historical value, and indeed, their own beauty. Slowly a campaign to halt the demolitions gathered momentum at first local and then national, culminating in 1973 when Adam Fergusson published his brilliant little polemic *The Sack of Bath*. It had a colossal and instantaneous impact on opinion throughout the country. The demolitions stopped and the City Council began to give the owners of these 'unimportant' houses the improvement grants which had been given to grander houses since 1955.

At the same time the Council began a project to restore the Circus façade. Severely eroded or lost ornaments were re-carved, soot washed away and paint removed from stonework. In the more prosperous 1970s this encouraged the owners of houses in the more notable terraces to form residents' associations, which, for example, restored the wrought-iron overthrows and lamps in Lansdown Crescent, and replaced the railings in the squares. In 1983 the National Trust bought the woods and fields on the hillsides forming the views to the east of the city. After an enormous cleaning programme, at last the city's stonework could be seen again. Limestone is, almost literally, fossilised sunshine, and no limestone appears to reflect this more than Bath stone, which glows even on dull days.

By the end of the century Bath had been utterly transformed. The turning point was the arrival of the University, eventually bringing an influx of 10,000 young people into the city of 80,000. The community was rejuvenated and given new energy. Today Bath again deserves the reputation which it squandered through the second half of the nineteenth century and the first half of the twentieth. Each year four and a half million people come from all over the world to see it.

Classical architecture is extremely fragile; alter one part and you damage the whole. The best definition of classical beauty is Alberti's famous paraphrase of the Roman architect Vitruvius: beauty is 'the harmony and concord of all the parts achieved in such a way that nothing can be added, taken away or altered, except for the worse'. The beauty of Bath resides mostly in its terraces, squares and crescents. All their constituent houses have been designed to give up their individuality to the greater whole. Alter one house and you damage the unity – the beauty – of the entire terrace.

Architecture is unlike most other forms of art in being made for use, much more than for the pleasure obtainable from its beauty. As any ancient church or house demonstrates, the way in which it is used *always* changes over time, often requiring alterations to its fabric. The beauty of a classical building, which cannot be altered except for the worse, is therefore much more fragile than that of a non-classical one, which can. As the Victorian Goths delighted to point out, a medieval building can be, and usually has been, altered and extended over centuries and looks all the better for it. That can be said of Bath's Abbey, but it can't be said of Milsom Street, which has been altered as fashion and social arrangements changed, and looks the worse for it.

Few changes are as damaging to the appearance of a classical building as a change of use, and of those the conversion of houses into shops has been the most common and usually the most devastating. In Milsom Street almost every house lost its ground floor in the nineteenth century when it was converted into a shop or a bank. Five of the houses, Somerset Buildings, are outstandingly fine. They were designed and built by the highly gifted Thomas Baldwin in 1781-3. By 1900 the frontage at ground level of four out of the five had been destroyed by their conversion into shops and a bank. Over the last forty years three of them have been restored, but even now, the more one appreciates the loveliness of the composition, the more one is distressed by what remains of its mutilation. (ill. 97) When looking at it, pleasure is always mixed with pain. The house next door has also lost its ground floor, but because it is not part of a great classical composition, the damage is painful but much less so than what has been done to its neighbours.

This sort of damage caused by the conversion of houses into shops is so common in Britain as to be routine, and so routine that we scarcely notice it. We are not unique, it occurs in every country old enough to have inherited buildings from the past and rich enough now to want to modernise them. But in France and Italy it occurs less often, for a very simple reason. There it has frequently been usual for apartment blocks and town houses – in Italy even some palaces of the nobility – to be designed from the start with shops on the ground floors. That has been much rarer here. Some originally classical streets, such as Oxford Street in London and Princes Street in Edinburgh, have been almost entirely rebuilt and have lost all their classical character. They stand as a constant reminder of how easily classical streets can transmute into ordinary ones. There are no examples yet of the process occurring in reverse. Perhaps one day it will. It is impossible and foolish to predict the future, but it may be that superstores, shopping-centres and on-line shopping will eventually kill the majority of small shops. Should that happen, domestic streets which have become shopping streets, could revert to their original purpose.

Subsequent changes are not the only disasters to which classical buildings are subject. Some were spoilt before they were even completed. An example is Prior Park. It was designed by John Wood for the wealthy Ralph Allen who, while it was being built, kept changing his mind about what he wanted, sometimes instructing the builders to make major changes without consulting poor Wood, who eventually resigned in disgust. The main change is that the great side wings were built asymmetrically. Subsequent alterations have made them a great deal worse, so that they no longer relate to the mansion in any visually meaningful way. The effect which Wood intended has been destroyed.

1 Early glazing bars, late 1720s.
Beauford Square

2 Regency glazing bars, 1804.
Sydney Place

Other sorts of changes have been inflicted on classical buildings that are not so immediately apparent. Some were so universal that we have become accustomed to them, even to the extent, occasionally, of preferring them. Windows have always been the most frequently altered external feature of a house. In the seventeenth century domestic windows were casements, often with a transom and a mullion forming a cross within the rectangular window opening. The glazing consisted of small rectangular or diamond-shaped pieces of glass held in lead cames. In about 1670 vertical sliding sashes with counter-balancing weights were invented in England. The limitations of glass blowing produced rectangular panes with a maximum economic dimension of not much more than a foot, so each sash had to be sub-divided by glazing bars. By just after 1700 sashes had become so fashionable that the majority of casement windows in polite houses, most of them in perfectly good condition, were taken out and replaced by sashes. It is very hard, when looking at buildings as familiar as Inigo Jones's Banqueting House in Whitehall or his Queen's House at Greenwich, to remember that their sashes are not original and that they once had mullioned and transomed casements. It is equally hard for us to believe that the appearance of either building was spoilt by the alteration, but it is unlikely that Inigo would agree. Glazing bars were usually, but not always, painted white. The compulsion to follow fashion or to stand conspicuously out from it caused occasional variations. In the 1830s there was a fashion for painting glazing bars olive green. A century earlier the enormously wealthy Thomas Coke had all the glazing bars in his new palace of Holkham gilded, and employed a full-time burnisher to keep them bright.

When sash windows were first introduced, joiners were not aware of how much stiffness the puttied sheets of glass would give to the wooden sashes. They consequently made the glazing bars about 50mm thick (1) which was ugly because their dark silhouette caused glare when looking out at a bright sky. Throughout the eighteenth century the thickness was whittled away, until by the Regency they were shaped like blades, only about 15mm thick. (2) This was optically superior because, having no surface parallel to the glass which would be seen in silhouette, their sides, especially if they were painted white, reflected the outside light, making them look brighter against the sky and causing much less glare. This practical advantage, plus the refinement resulting from their slenderness, caused the occupants of the huge majority of houses built in the earlier decades of the century to have their old glazing bars removed and replaced by more modern ones. Today one can often find the old bars remaining in unimportant windows, such as those in basements and attics.

In 1832 sheet glass was first manufactured in England, which allowed much larger panes than the older crown glass, and when it was greatly improved in 1838 people began to remove their glazing bars altogether. Only two years later, in 1840, relatively cheap plate glass was produced which was free of the ripples that distorted the view seen through crown glass.[1] Architects immediately took it up, and its appearance in new buildings finally made glazing bars in older houses seem hopelessly old fashioned. Anybody with the faintest pretensions to good taste felt compelled to remove them from the windows on the front of their houses, and often from all sides, and replace them with a single sheet of plate glass in each sash. (3) In recent decades the process has gone into reverse and the plate glass is being removed and the glazing bars put back again. Few people realise just how universal these changes were: in the Royal Crescent, for instance, every house except two had the glazing bars removed from the windows in its front, and in the last fifty or sixty years about half have been put back again. It is at least possible (though perhaps unlikely) that John Wood, the architect of Royal Crescent, and the architects who designed the thousands of other houses in Britain that lost their glazing bars, would not have been too upset about this, because the overall proportions of the façade were unaffected. It seems that architects at Wood's time did not consider a window's subdivision into panes to be very significant because when they prepared their elevation drawings they rarely drew them, usually showing the window openings as dark rectangles, with no attempt to show the window frames or the glazing bars. That was also the case in most engraved elevations in the architectural books of the time. (18) By the 1770s that had changed and glazing bars were usually indicated, probably because the architects wanted to ensure that when the joiners made them, the proportions of the individual panes would relate harmoniously to the proportions of the façades. (92)

3 John Wood's houses in Queen Square. In some windows the glazing bars have been removed and others have been elongated

Architects of the mid-century terraces would certainly have hated another change that later taste inflicted on their windows. In the Romantic years approaching 1800 people wanted to be in the closest possible contact with nature and the outside world. They began to explore

---

1 From the seventeenth century plate glass, sometimes in very large sheets, was made for use in mirrors and occasionally in windows, but it was extremely expensive because it had to be laboriously ground down and polished by hand. In 1827 the millionaire William Beckford removed the glazing bars from his two houses in Lansdown Crescent and inserted plate glass. It was not until after 1840 that many of his neighbours could afford to follow his lead.

the Wye valley, the Lake District and the Scottish Highlands, and rhapsodised over their wild and picturesque scenery. Previously, large houses had all their reception rooms on the first floor, the piano nobile. In the second half of the century this became unacceptable and people moved downstairs to live on the ground floor. By 1790 or so, new country houses and villas were being designed with French doors so that occupants could step directly into their gardens, or bring them indoors with potted plants. Conservatories accessible from the main rooms became a necessity. In towns, however, most people lived in terrace houses where none of this was possible. Restricted space meant that the kitchens and pantries had to be in the basement, which in turn meant that there had to be sunk areas at front and back to light and ventilate them; in effect a dry moat separating the house from the garden and the street. Dining rooms were usually located on the ground floor to be near the kitchen and the servants below, so drawing rooms had to be on the first floor. The desire for close contact with nature had to be satisfied by having the newly developed iron balconies fixed onto the sunny side of the house, or balconettes which could then be furnished with potted plants. Balconies required that the window cills had to be lowered to near floor level so that people could step into them. Other people realised that if the drawing-room windows were extended down to the floor and the sashes opened to their fullest extent, the room itself would become an equivalent to a balcony. Any of this was a great deal more expensive than altering the glazing bars, but many who could afford to do so altered their house in one or other of these ways. To take the Royal Crescent as an example again, every house had the first-floor windows in its south front extended in this way, though respect for the famous façade inhibited the occupants from attaching balconies. Only one house, number 1, has had the original proportions of its windows restored. In the early nineteenth century many of the windows in the Circus were given iron balconettes, all of them of different design. Most of them are still there.

Many of the less famous terraces were treated with scarcely any respect at all. An example is Marlborough Buildings, which has had almost every indignity heaped upon it. When it was built in about 1789, the cills of the first-floor windows were continued across the façade of each house, a feature called a cill-band. Within a year or two some of its first-floor windows had been lengthened, leaving the remains of the cill-bands as meaningless horizontal lines between the windows. An 1801 engraving (by Jacob Spornberg) shows that none of the houses had balconies at that date. In the next few decades a miscellaneous collection of them were added to most of the houses, and in one house a balcony has been subsequently removed, leaving ugly scars. At the northern end of the terrace a motley collection of bathroom extensions were built onto the façades in the decades around 1900. The result is an appalling mess. These things, or some of them, were inflicted on terraces all over the city.

It might seem strange that architects and their clients should go on building classical terraces and streets when it was so likely that eventually they would be altered and therefore spoilt. It was never for lack of an alternative, because the enormously vigorous and attractive High Street tradition, where every building is unique, was always available. Streets in this huge category, which don't merely accept change but thrive on it, have their own delights but they clearly lack whatever it is that makes people want to build classical streets.

There is no doubt about what that is. People delight in variety, but they also have a deep need for order. The variety of the High Street is an expression of individual freedom: the classical street is an expression of social and civic order. It is this that is at the heart of mankind's recurring urge to build ordered streets and ordered cities. But wherever in the world the architecture of ancient Rome has exerted its strange but irresistible compulsion, streets that derive their order from classicism have had an even greater power.

The essence of the classical system of architecture has always been seen as the five orders; the three main or Greek orders, Doric, Ionic and Corinthian, and the two subsequent or Roman orders, Tuscan and Composite. Some people, such as Sir Isaac Newton and after him John Wood, believed that the orders were divinely ordained, and given to mankind at the building of Moses' Tabernacle and the Temple in Jerusalem. It would doubtless be possible to invent an entirely new system of architectural design which would have most of the advantages of the classical orders, and even perhaps a few in addition. But it could not have what is now classical architecture's greatest advantage: that it has moved and inspired people for two and a half thousand years, longer even than Christianity. The longer it survives the more potent it becomes. It is not merely a symbol of social and civic order; it has become, for those who love it, a paradigm of order itself, the basis of everything.

2 Aquae Sulis

Bath, Aquae Sulis, the leading spa of Roman Britain, was a small town of little significance otherwise. Its great importance in subsequent history, apart from the purely archaeological, lies in the fact that in the early eighteenth century a local builder's son, knowing nothing whatever about Roman Bath beyond the fact that it had existed, used this knowledge to build in his imagination the great dream city he believed Bath must have been, and then set out to recreate it. His name, as everybody knows, was John Wood. His buildings caught the nation's attention and initiated the growth of the enchanting classical city we have inherited.

Bath's beginnings were back in the Iron Age when Celts began to settle in the vicinity of the three geo-thermal springs. The miraculous delivery of hot water from the earth's womb was clearly the gift of a goddess, whom they called Sulis. Even today the springs are awe-inspiring. The one which was later to serve the King's Bath produces almost a quarter of a million gallons of water a day at a temperature of 46°C, the Hot Bath spring emerges at a temperature of 49°C, and the Cross Bath spring at 40°C, the water having fallen as rain up to 8,000 years ago, then sunk into the earth and percolated between hot plates of rock two miles below the surface.

It is known that there was a Celtic settlement on the well-drained land at Walcot, but how far it extended into the later town area is uncertain. It is also known that there was an ancient ford over the Avon just below the present site of Cleveland Bridge. The land around the springs would have been shrouded in steam and almost impassably marshy, but archaeologists have discovered traces of a rubble causeway giving access to the King's Bath spring. Whether there was some sort of associated shrine is not known.

Bath emerged into events in recorded history after the Roman invasion of AD 43. Its first mention in literature, as Aquae Calidae, the Hot Waters, was recorded in about 150 by the Alexandrian geographer Claudius Ptolemy. A century later, in about 250, Gaius Julius Solinus wrote of it: 'there are hot springs lavishly fitted out for human use. Their presiding deity is Minerva, and in her temple the ever-burning fires never whiten away into ashes, but when the flame dies down the fire turns into rocky lumps.' In the accommodating Roman way Sulis had been conflated with Minerva, the nearest Roman equivalent. The fuel which was apparently unknown to Solinus was Somerset coal.

The occupying army's first task was the building of a network of roads across the country, guarded by a chain of wild-west type wooden forts, one of which may have been at Bathwick where Samian pottery shards have been found. The Fosseway, running from Dorset to Lincolnshire, crossed the Avon at Bath, and linked there with the road to the port of Abona (now Sea Mills, near Bristol). After the suppression of Queen Boudicca's revolt in AD 60 the Romans began a national programme of public building. Although Bath was very small and not one of the new cantonal capitals, the number of visitors to its hot springs was already sufficient to prompt the erection of a monumental bath complex. Before construction began the engineers trapped the spring with the largest flow in a polygonal lead-lined reservoir, thus allowing the surrounding marsh to dry out. The outflow was

channelled into the river. When the land was dry enough to support buildings, construction of the bath complex could proceed. It consisted of a large rectangular entrance hall which probably at that stage functioned as a frigidarium, as it certainly did later. On its short north side were three arches looking out to the Sacred Spring in its basin. Opposite, on the western side, were a small calidarium and a tepidarium, warm rooms heated by hypocausts below their floors. (4) A heap of cinders unearthed in 1895 suggests that they were probably fuelled by coal. On the east side was the great hall in the centre of which was the warm swimming pool fed by the Sacred Spring and lined with thick sheets of lead. Arising out of the pool were the plinths which survive today. (Everything above that low level which the visitor sees today was built in 1895 and bears no relation to what originally existed.) The plinths supported an arcade running around the pool, with a two-storey enclosing wall with lunette windows above it. Set back behind the arcade were wide single-storey walkways, and behind them large alcoves for seating. At that stage the great hall was timber roofed, which was bad practice because dry rot, probably unknown to the Romans, was inevitable in the bath's warm moist atmosphere. Later the roof had to be replaced by a concrete vault. Beyond the hall was another, smaller pool.

Over their remaining 300-odd years of use the baths were constantly repaired, altered and extended, becoming finally a large complex of bath buildings and temples. According to the archaeologist Barry Cunliffe, 'it would have been then, as it is now, one of the wonders of Roman Britain'.

The Baths were essentially religious. The complex was so arranged that every time bathers visited the building for its recreational and therapeutic activities they first saw the Sacred Spring welling up in its great basin. They saw more than that. The long axis of the Bath's rectangular entrance hall passed through the central arch of its north wall, then through the Sacred Spring, on through a narrow opening into a large colonnaded courtyard in which it finally focussed on the large carved stone altar dedicated to the Goddess. At a right angle to this north-south

5 Model of the Roman
Baths in the Baths
Museum

axis was another which focussed at its east end on the altar, and at its west end on the
tetrastyle (four column) portico of a small Corinthian temple raised on a podium about 4.5m
high and approached by a flight of steps. (5) The pediment was filled with a carved relief of a
gorgon's head in a circular wreath of oak leaves, supported by winged victories. (The temple
was below what is now Stall Street.) Only fragments of all this survive, but enough to make
possible a fairly reliable restoration. The largest decorative fragments are the pediment
sculptures. (6) In 1913 a convincing replica temple was built in Sydney Gardens when they
were opened as a public park. Unfortunately the replica does not have the high podium or
great flight of steps. (7) Examination of the genuine fragments in the Baths Museum reveal
that the design and workmanship were provincial – the gorgon is crudely carved, the column
bases are clumsy, and so on, but the overall effect must have been splendid.

The eternal flame and a statue of Minerva would have been in the temple's cella, the room at
the back which was accessible only to the priests. Their public functions, such as making
animal sacrifices at the altar, were in the open where they could be seen by the people. That
there was a male Gorgon's head in the pediment of a temple dedicated to the female Sul
Minerva is an unexplained puzzle, as is the meaning of the male and female figures at each of
the four corners of the great altar. In 1727 workmen digging a trench for a sewer in Stall Street
found the famous gilt bronze life-size head of Minerva. It is assumed that the statue of which
she was part came from the temple. She was presumably decapitated and her now missing

helmet wrenched off by Christian zealots after the temple and the old religion were abandoned. The head is beautiful but like the temple and baths clearly of provincial workmanship, probably Gaulish. No Roman work of art of really high quality has been found in Bath.

Over the 300 years of its existence, the bath and temple complex was extended and the early structures altered. The basin holding the Sacred Spring, for example, was enclosed in a vaulted hall. In the great court several small altars were erected, two of them positioned to emphasise its east-west axis. They were housed in little classical buildings on either side of the steps going up to the temple, and thus framing it. The details may have been a little crude, but the effect must have been glorious.

The complex finally became quite large, but on nothing remotely like the scale of the great Baths in Rome. The Baths of Caracalla, for instance, were an immense complex of towering halls, courts and rooms, all of different complex shapes, all linked on numerous crossing axes revealing great vistas of columns, arches and spaces receding into the distance. Aquae Sulis's much more modest version declined in the fourth century when prosperous Britain was increasingly attacked by barbarian raiders from northern Europe seeking plunder. The many villas in the surrounding countryside were abandoned and their residents sought refuge in the walled town. Then that too succumbed. Bath was looted and its remaining inhabitants could no longer afford to carry out repairs. The land around the springs reverted to marsh. The buildings decayed and until they collapsed were occupied by generations of squatters. When civilisation at last returned, successive generations of buildings were erected on top of the rubble until the Roman street level was 12 feet below ground. The historic reality was lost, but the legend and the dream remained.

6 Gorgon's Head from the temple of Sul Minerva's pediment

7 The 1913 replica temple of Sul Minerva in Sydney Gardens

3 Bath before John Wood

Bath stepped back into history in the sixth century when the Abbey was founded as a Benedictine monastery. In the late ninth century King Alfred repaired the city walls and laid out a new road pattern on top of the buried Roman one. In 959 Edgar was crowned in the Abbey as the first King of all England. In 1075 it was decreed that the sees of bishops should if possible be in the more populous towns, so the Bishop of Wells transferred to Bath, demolished the Saxon Abbey and rebuilt it on a huge scale. To recompense the disgruntled canons of Wells, in 1244 the see was renamed Bath and Wells. In the sixteenth century the Norman Abbey church having become derelict, it was replaced by a third version, the much smaller present one. As it was an abbey it was dissolved in 1539 and sold. The new owner stripped the roof and sold whatever materials he could. It was decaying and open to the elements for several decades.

At the start of the eighteenth century Bath was an ordinary little country town, most of it still within its largely surviving town wall. It was known outside Somerset only for its therapeutic hot springs and the bizarre fact that half a bishop gave it the status of a city. It had a population of two or three thousand people, most of them employed on weaving woolen cloth or working it. A map of 1694 had drawings of the city's most notable houses engraved in its margins.[1] Some were newish, some quite ancient and some of imposing size, but not one was classical. Of the 36 depicted, only one survives in the rebuilt city today. All the larger houses in the city, and most of the lesser ones, were built of the local stone and roofed with the local stone tiles. In 1654 John Evelyn spent four days in Bath where he recorded that 'the towne is intirely built of stone, but the streets narrow, uneven and unpleasant'. Like all visitors he missed the slums, where the tightly crowded hovels, as John Wood called them, were probably built of timber and certainly roofed with thatch, the cause of occasional fires. There was nothing unusual about any of this, most country towns in stone districts will have been roughly similar. Fourteen years later Pepys and his wife visited Bath, and in the socially relaxed seventeenth-century way brought their servants to share the holiday. Pepys found the 'town most of stone and clean though the streets generally narrow.' 'Up at 4 a'clock being by appointment called up to the Bath where we were carried after one another ... And by and by ... came much company very fine ladies and the manner pretty enough only methinks it cannot be clean to go so many bodies together in to the same water. ... Strange to see how hot the water is and in some places though this is the most temperate bath the springs so hot as the feet not to endure. ... Carried back wrap in a sheet and in a chair home and there one after another thus carried (I staying above two hours in the water) home to bed sweating for an hour and by and by comes music to play to me extraordinary good as ever I heard at London almost anywhere'. He recorded that the visit to Bath cost him five shillings.

[1] This was a common way of subsidising the cost of surveying and printing a map. Owners of the houses depicted were expected to make a generous contribution.

Many visitors were West Country squires and their families, but a considerable number, like Pepys, came from further away, and some like Evelyn, from grander social strata. Even royals came occasionally. Queen Elizabeth came in 1574 on one of her constant progresses around the country, and her criticism of the citizens having allowed the Abbey to become roofless and tumbledown jolted them into beginning its repair. Later, in 1590, she gave the city its charter formally incorporating it and extending its boundaries down to the river's loop and uphill to include the rural parish of Walcot, the eventual site of John Wood's great developments. James I's Queen came three times, the small bath beside the larger King's Bath being named the Queen's Bath in her honour. In 1663 Charles II, in desperate need of a legitimate heir, brought his Queen to bathe in the waters which claimed to promote fecundity as well as curing skin diseases, gout and almost everything else. It didn't work for her but it did for James II's Queen, who soon after her visit became pregnant. Nor did it work for poor Queen Anne, who came twice, in 1702 and 1703, desperately seeking a cure for the dropsy aggravated by gout which killed her. She said the waters gave her some relief, but it was the usual triumph of hope over reality. Royals and aristocrats on their visits could stay with local grandees in the surrounding countryside, but the lodgings for everybody else were too crude, too few and therefore expensive. Their rents started to make Bath prosperous but not yet fashionable.

Most visitors are unlikely to have spent much longer bathing in the waters than Pepys's two hours (drinking them probably hadn't yet started), so inevitably they filled their time playing cards, dancing and gambling. All this was controlled by a Master of Ceremonies appointed by the City Council. A very remarkable young man called Richard Nash, guessing that Queen Anne's visits would improve Bath's social position, decided to try his luck there. He had enormous charm and was socially acceptable, coming from what was then called a 'respectable' but not distinguished Welsh family. After matriculating from Jesus College, Oxford, he entered the Inner Temple but soon realised that a lifetime as a lawyer was not for him. He even spent a short time in the army, but had discovered that his high intelligence enabled him to earn a decent living from gambling. This and his notable charm and wit soon obtained him the position of assistant to the Master of Ceremonies, and his gambler's luck soon obtained him the post itself when the incumbent was killed in a duel. Nash, more than anybody else, made Bath fashionable and prosperous. He was a notably ugly man, but made up for it by a style of dress of compensating magnificence, so much so that he became known universally as Beau Nash. He soon took an autocratic but benevolent control of the evening Assemblies, introducing a code of polite behaviour which was long overdue in England, publicly reprimanding aristocrats who refused to dance with social inferiors, and on one occasion even rebuking a duchess for being incorrectly dressed. By the 1720s he had made it fashionable and not merely therapeutic to visit Bath, so that regular or occasional visits by families throughout the kingdom had become socially almost essential, causing a mixing in public assemblies of the middling and upper classes that was new in England but unknown in Paris, St Petersburg or other great European cities.

8 The Saracen's Head, Broad Street. c.1700

The increasing number of visitors required a lot of new lodgings. Not many built before about 1700 were to survive the great rebuilding that was soon to begin, so they are now uncommon in Bath. Many of them will have been in a vernacular similar to the gabled Saracen's Head in Broad Street, one of the survivors which probably dates from about 1700. (8) The turn of the century was a fascinating moment of transition in English street architecture. Until then most vernacular buildings had been gabled, which is the logical method of terminating pitched roofs. Most contemporary depictions of seventeenth-century towns show the streets to have consisted of rows of gabled houses, although the much more sophisticated and aristocratic buildings of Wren, Vanbrugh and their associates and followers, like their sixteenth- and seventeenth-century Italian models, always had flat-topped fronts where the roofs sloped down to gutters hidden behind parapets. This construction was not logical: it was much more expensive than gables, and unless the gutters were annually cleared of dead leaves, they were liable to overflow their lead upstand flashings and flood through the ceilings. Parapets had little practical advantage, but in the years around 1700 they became irresistibly fashionable, and high fashion is never deterred by impracticality. So gables became more or less extinct in the prosperous areas of towns, not to be revived until the nineteenth century saw them with new eyes. But in the decades after 1700 they seemed so embarrassingly old-fashioned that one occasionally sees seventeenth-century houses where the pitched roofs were cut back a few feet and the house re-fronted with a flat-topped façade.

This development coincided with another which was mentioned in the first chapter – the sudden fashion for counter-balanced sliding sashes. It isn't possible to know whether the Saracen's Head originally had casements or its present sashes when it was built. What is certain is that its glazing bars are too slim to be original. Until the nineteenth century glass was blown by mouth and the resultant small panes had to be held in the sash by glazing bars or, in earlier years, lead cames. The earliest glazing bars were very heavy, but throughout the eighteenth century became thinner and thinner. Soon the early bars looked crude and they in turn had to be replaced. In the Saracen's Head the bars are of intermediate thickness, and therefore either mid-century replacements of earlier bars, or the windows are mid-century replacements of casements. The latter seems the more probable. One little detail which couldn't easily be altered is, with the gables, the most reliable clue to the date of this building – the heavily projecting bolection mouldings around the entrance and the first-floor windows, a feature which was popular with builders for a few decades around 1700.

By 1700 visitors to Bath were being encouraged to drink the spa water, so in 1706 a now lost Pump Room was built, with taps connected to the spring. People assembled to drink, chat and listen to music. This early Pump Room was probably the first fully classical building in the city since the fourth century. Its entrance front consisted of four high-arched openings, the piers between them having attached Corinthian half columns with their correct entablatures breaking forward over them. The slightly wider south-facing back had five arches divided by Doric half columns. John Wood rarely praised other men's work, but he did record his approval of this building, which he tells us was built and designed by the younger John Harvey.[2] It would be fascinating to know where Harvey picked up his knowledge of classical design. The Pump Room soon becoming over-crowded, in 1708 the first Assembly Room was built (by an unknown architect). Beau Nash was setting a cracking pace. The Assembly Room was simple with few architectural pretensions, but remained in use for well over a century, co-existing with the younger John Wood's larger and more magnificent Assembly Rooms of 1771 which survive today. The old one was finally demolished in 1933.

9 General Wolfe's House in Trim Street, c.1720

Two ambitious houses of about 1720 survive, both coincidentally known by the name of alleged later occupants, both of them generals. One, in Trim Street, is now known as General Wolfe's House. (9) It has none of the classical purity of the Pump Room, being crammed with incident. The windows, which sit on moulded aprons, have deeply projecting bolection-moulded architraves and obviously later glazing bars. The doorway has deeply fluted Ionic pilasters and a segmental pediment. On the floor above, the central window is framed by two more fluted pilasters, this time Corinthian, supporting a second segmental pediment curved more steeply than the one below. Wood and his fellow Palladians doubtless considered it all laughably incorrect and provincial.

General Wade's House of about the same date, has a handsome cheerily ignorant façade which does a lot to enliven Abbey Churchyard. (10) It is unfortunate that it has lost its ground floor, but impossible to regret it very much because in about 1820 it was replaced by the present lovely Regency shopfront. The loss is serious however because it means that the heavy pilasters have nothing visually strong enough to support them, and it is impossible now to know how the unknown designer organised the façade as a whole. The façade is a lesson to pedants, demonstrating how irrelevant the rules of classical design can sometimes be: it seems to have been designed to break as many rules as possible and yet is somehow very attractive. There are four bays and five pilasters instead of the canonical odd number of bays and even number

2 There were three John Harveys, presumably father, son and grandson. The Pump Room was built by the son. The now lost church of St Michael in Bath, of 1734, was built by one of the Harveys, presumably the grandson. One of the family, presumably the father, worked as a sculptor at Longleat between 1687 and 1701, and there are monuments by one or other of them in several west country churches, including Bath Abbey.

10 General Wade's House,
c.1720, in Abbey
Churchyard.
Shopfront c.1820

THE CLASSICAL BUILDINGS OF BATH

11 Beauford Square.
John Strahan, late 1720s.
The two central houses
have subsequently been
given upper floors

of pilasters; the pedestals are too small to support such weighty pilasters; the first and second floor windows are of equal size, giving undue prominence to the bedroom windows and not enough to those of the reception rooms; the attic looks like an afterthought; the vases on the parapet are too small and the Ionic capitals distressingly so. Does any of this matter? It did, very much, to the following generation who were fighting for the introduction of what they believed to be true classicism to Britain. Does it matter to us? No: in architecture the eyes have it and ours are not dimmed by eighteenth-century spectacles.

Two residential squares were built in these late 1720s, Kingsmead and Beauford, both designed by the architect John Strahan (? - c1740). Kingsmead Square never had much unity and today is an architectural confusion, but the houses in Beauford Square (some of them now a faithful modern rebuilding) have great charm and, considering their tiny size, a surprising dignity, due in large measure to their Doric entablatures. (11) Even Wood, after referring to Strahan's 'Piratical Architecture', had to admit that these houses 'far exceed the common Buildings of any Place that I have yet seen', and 'have a Sort of Regularity to recommend them'. His dislike of Strahan was undoubtedly motivated by professional jealousy,[3] but it had a deeper basis: Wood was a Palladian and Strahan was not, though towards the end of his life he tried to adopt this latest fashion. (His Redland Court and Chapel in Bristol were stumbling attempts at it, but despite its faults the Court is pleasing and the Chapel superb, the best eighteenth-century church in Bristol.) Strahan, like the designer of General Wade's House, had been brought up

3 In the third edition of his *Essay*, long after Strahan's death, Wood dropped his reference to piratical architecture. Strahan was no longer a rival.

12 Widcombe Manor,
1726-7. (Photo M Jenner)

at a time when there were fewer architectural rules: it is almost true to say that if something looked good it was good enough.

Some of Palladio's rules, extracted from his study of Vitruvius and surviving Roman buildings, turned out to be so restrictive that they were silently dropped, for instance his statement that the metopes in Doric entablatures had to be square. Even he ignored that when it suited him. But that apart, the discipline of the Doric entablature was sacrosanct, and it made the design of Doric façades extremely demanding because it dictated the spacing of all its elements. Where there were columns, a triglyth *had* to be positioned centrally over each one, and either a triglyth or a metope *had* to be positioned centrally over each door or window. Because the triglyths and metopes had to have equal spacing across the façade, they, and not convenience, dictated the precise position of each window, door or arch. The Beauford houses had a Doric entablature but no columns, which was questionable though not exactly illicit, but the spacing of the elements in the entablature bore no relationship to the spacing of the windows, which was unforgivable. To Strahan triglyths were simply ornaments, no more. He obviously thought they gave his rows of small houses a little dignity. That they should be the basis of an entire system of ordering never entered his mind. Even today, to those few who notice it, such sloppy design is jarring. Apart from that minor irritation the façades are splendid.

Widcombe Manor was built towards the end of the seventeenth century, but was much altered and given new west and south fronts in 1726-7. (12) The windows in the west front's bay window have obviously been subsequently lengthened down to the floor, probably at the end of the eighteenth century, but the south front appears to be original. In some ways its design is admirable, but the usual pre-Palladian over-crowding is unfortunate. The façade is organised into a wide central pavilion and narrower side wings, with pairs of giant Ionic pilasters sitting on a semi-basement. The Doric entrance doorway (with its triglyths properly distributed, unlike those in Beauford Square) has a segmental pediment. Above it the wall breaks forward a few inches to continue the line of the porch upward. Squeezed between the porch and the nearest pilasters are narrow arched windows set in a few inches of rusticated stone, which is also used at first-floor level. In the side wings the windows are framed in the bolection moulding, still, in 1726, being used by artisan designers. The windows, with typically large baroque keystones, seem to be jostled by the giant pilasters. Most of these unhappy details could have been improved by a better informed designer, but the big things in this façade are successful: the golden Bath stone; the projecting porch; the giant pilasters sitting on the semi-basement; the modillioned cornice and pediment; the bull's eye window and its festoon in the pediment; the up-to-the-minute Palladian balustrade and the glorious stone-tiled roof. It is only when one looks closely that the defects become apparent. With all its faults this is a highly enjoyable façade, but it is provincial, rustic. If Richard Strauss's Baron Ochs had been English, one could imagine him living here.

The façades of the Wolfe and Widcombe houses would have looked happier if their designers had known more about the rules of design which accompanied classicism. Even to have done what they did required a considerable amount of knowledge, which they could get easily from one of the many books on the orders. Designers had to know about the proportions of each column and those of its base and entablature, and how to draw them. With their books beside their drawing boards this was not difficult. It was the more subtle rules that defeated them. A highly intelligent and creative architect such as Robert Adam could break rules when he needed, because what he produced by doing so was self evidently an adequate justification. (Not everybody agreed; in the nineteenth century he was increasingly criticised for this.) The rules were based on the fact that some things look better than others, and rules which helped achieve them made success more probable and failure less likely. Later the rules became too rigid, and new ones, often unwritten, were added to the number. Architecture, like most human activity, is subject to fashion, and fashion changes every few decades as each generation recognises the absurdities and disadvantages of the work of their fathers and grandfathers. In the 1720s the pendulum of fashion was making one of its great swings. Buildings like General Wade's House seemed laughable to John Wood's generation, just as in the 1760s the return swing would make Wood's early work seem crude and old-fashioned. Following the swing of the pendulum will be one of the minor themes of this book. The metaphor is not exact because real pendulums always go back to where they were before. Fashion never does, but it *always* goes back near enough to allow each new generation to appreciate the work of their grandfathers that their fathers had despised, and it compels them to react against the work of their fathers.

The Wade façade is an example of this. The Palladians laughed at the festoons under the windows and were horrified at the odd number of pilasters, but in the 1760s and 1770s, attitudes changed. Robert Adam re-introduced festoons, and some of his followers even used an odd number of pilasters when it suited them. They would have considered the Wade façade clumsy and over-emphatic, but they would have been much more indulgent to it than their fathers would have been. Earlier in the century the pendulum had swung against Sir Christopher Wren when he was old and finishing St Paul's. By then the Palladians considered his design to be old-fashioned, so he was replaced by a younger man and a 'correct' Palladian balustrade put on the parapet. Wren was heartbroken. The same process occurred when the Victorians reacted against 'boring' Georgian terraces; when the 1920s reacted against Victorian 'ugliness'; when the 1960s rediscovered the glory of Victorian design; and it is happening now when everybody dismisses buildings of the 1960s and 1970s as 'brutal' and 'inhuman'. The reaction against that is already beginning, with even a few of the tower blocks having been listed as worthy of preservation. So it goes on, and so it always will. The rejection of their fathers' values by the young is cruel but probably biologically necessary.

Rosewell House in Kingsmead Square is a building which can help explain why the Palladians reacted against the crowded façades of the early 1700s. (13) It was completed in 1735, as recorded beside Thomas Rosewell's rebus of a rose and a well under the pediment. It was therefore contemporary with John Wood's Queen Square which was completed in the following year. They stand at opposite architectural poles. The house was almost certainly designed by Nathaniel Ireson, architect, master builder, quarry owner, and proprietor of a delftware pottery. In his youth he had worked as an assistant to Francis Smith of Warwick and Thomas Archer, the latter of whom had the greatest influence on him. Archer, a wealthy gentleman architect, had travelled abroad for four years and is the only major English architect to show the direct influence of Borromini and the architecture of Germany and Austria. These baroque influences, never popular in England and much derided throughout the eighteenth and nineteenth centuries, are powerfully reflected at Rosewell House.

Like General Wade's House, Rosewell's has lost its ground floor to shops, which make it impossible to know for certain how the façade was ordered. The surviving entrance porch, which contains the only columns on the façade, seems stylistically unrelated to the rest of the front, being much simpler. The elliptically arched window above it is a riot of baroque ornament, with Germanic or Flemish terms[4] flanking it, and the window above has great swirling festoons cascading down each side. Its exaggeratedly huge keystone pushes the Rosewell rebus up into the elliptical pediment. To either side of this wide central bay are the narrower outer bays with two windows on each floor. Those on the first floor are framed by eared architraves which continue above the windows as a sort of elliptical pediment broken

4 Terms, a Roman invention, are tapered pedestals terminating at the top as human busts.

13 Rosewell House,
Kingsmead Square. 1735

by keystones carved with emblems of the four seasons. They and the terms would look at home in Vienna but seem very foreign in Bath. The windows on the top floor are unmistakably Borrominian, but Borromini filtered through Vanbrugh and Archer. Their eared architraves follow the general pattern of those on the floor below, but without curves or carved ornament. Above them are crushingly heavy features called tables carrying scrolls supporting the cornice.

Ireson was much more scholarly here than the unknown designers of the houses described earlier, but the combination of his features, each of them 'correct', is clumsy. (We must remember that it is impossible to be sure of this because the vital ground floor is missing. The surviving rusticated piers at that level hint that the lower storey of the side bays may also have been rusticated, thus providing a heavy base for the outer bays which may have pulled everything together.) It is easy to understand how Wood and his generation hated this building. The beautifully calm elevations of Palladio were so familiar to them (in Wood's case only through engravings: he never went to Italy) that Palladio had become one of them, almost an honorary Englishman. Rosewell's details, which Wood called 'ornaments without taste' were foreign, un-English.[5] One has only to look at the north side of Queen Square, or any other of the great achievements of the English Palladians, to see how outrageous Rosewell House's crammed façade must have seemed. But it was not only the cramming, all Palladian façades are ordered by a coherent system of proportioning: they sing. It is that hidden but always sensed harmony of proportion which, more than anything else, has made Georgian architecture so much loved in this country. There is no sense of that in the façade of Rosewell House.

So what was Palladianism? The designers of all the buildings except the Saracen's Head which have been described so far, obviously knew quite a lot about the Doric and Ionic orders to have been able to build them so convincingly. We know from whom Nathaniel Ireson got his knowledge, but the others almost certainly got theirs from books, of which at this date there were translations into English from Italian, French and Flemish originals, all plentifully illustrated with wood or copper engravings. At that period the most important of these were the books of Sebastiano Serlio (1475-1554) which were hugely influential in England and France (where he died). From the later Palladian point of view this was not entirely beneficial because artisan designers tended to pick on Serlio's more flamboyantly Mannerist illustrations, as the builder of Rosewell House had done. After 1700 his influence in England waned quickly, to be superseded by that of Andrea Palladio (1508-80).

Palladio was one of the greatest Italian architects, and the first to earn his reputation entirely from his architectural work, not also from painting or sculpture. Like all his professional contemporaries he was fascinated by the ruins of ancient Rome and spent much time travelling around Italy to study and measure them in order to ascertain the theory behind them. He was thoroughly familiar with Vitruvius's *De Architectura*, the only architectural treatise to survive from antiquity, which despite its obscurity gave him a solid base for his researches. He published several books but the most important was his *Quattro Libri dell' Architettura* of 1570 which was twenty years in the writing and became the most influential book in the history of architecture. He said of himself that he was a man of few words and his Four Books (in fact the four sections of one slim volume) are admirably terse, clear and readable. The book contains guidance on such practical matters as foundations, vaults etc. and then gives a full explanation of the five orders, Tuscan, Doric, Ionic, Corinthian and Composite. They are followed by descriptions of many of his own buildings and his conject-

5 This English naturalisation of the Italian renaissance masters was not limited to Wood's generation. The architect Sir Reginald Blomfield in his 1940 biography of Norman Shaw lamented that the tutelage of Bramante and Palladio was being superseded by foreigners. He meant Le Corbusier, Walter Gropius *et al.*

ural restorations of the Roman buildings he had surveyed. All of this is copiously illustrated by many wood engravings. His book established for all time the principle that architectural practice must be based on a firm foundation of theory.

The engravings of Palladio's own buildings reveal his passion for symmetry and his disposition of rooms proportioned to those next to them. Like all Italian architects since Alberti he believed that harmonious proportions were the basis of beauty in everything. In the first century BC Vitruvius, doubtless reflecting earlier Greek beliefs, wrote that the classical orders were based on human proportions. Leonardo had investigated the proportions of the ideal human body, which he found to produce ratios of 1:3, 1:2 and 1: 1 (the span of a man's outstretched arms is equal to his height). Countless scholars, going back to antiquity, had spent an enormous amount of energy investigating the arithmetical basis of musical harmony and it had been realised that the same rules applied to architecture. Palladio wrote 'the proportions of voices are harmonies for the ear; those of measurements are harmonies for the eyes. Such harmonies are very pleasing without anyone knowing why, except students of the causality of things'.

Palladio used simple numerical ratios in his buildings. He considered that the most noble spaces were the circle and the square, (1:1) but others should have proportions of 3:4 (a square and a third), 2:3 (a square and a half), 3:5 (a square and two thirds), and 1:2 (two squares). He lived almost all his life in Vicenza and the plans engraved in his book are carefully dimensioned in Vicentine feet so that architects could see how he had designed his villas and palaces in sequences of apartments of varying size but of the proportions he had recommended. In his First Book he says, 'I like those rooms very much whose length is two thirds more than the breadth, that is, if the breadth be eighteen feet, the length should be thirty'. He also gives rules for the height of rooms: 'if with a flat ceiling, their height ... must be equal to their breadth.' He gives other rules for vaulted rooms. His rule for the heights of windows in a façade are that they should diminish by a sixth on each storey.

The rules I have quoted are very simple, but there were others for particular circumstances that were more complicated, but explained so clearly that architects could follow them easily. The result of all this is that everything in his buildings is harmonically related to everything else, right down to the columns, their diameter at the foot being the module which sets the dimensions for all their parts and thence for the whole building. As he wrote, nobody recognises these relationships without measuring them, but everybody finds their result pleasing. Palladio's influence and his rules spread across Europe and eventually America, but took firmest hold in Britain. The practice of architecture had become a matter of books, of study, in addition to tutelage. The gulf between the trained craftsman and the educated architect had been established. It would widen and eventually be almost unbridgeable.

In 1715 the first expensive folio volume of a highly influential book was published in London, Colen Campbell's *Vitruvius Britannicus*, consisting of superb very large copper engravings of recent buildings, most of them at least tinged with the baroque, but including 18 plates of his own Palladian designs (none of them executed). They gave subscribers the first convenient opportunity to study the latest architectural fashion. In the same year Giacomo Leoni began publication of an English translation of Palladio's *Four Books*, with the original wood engravings re-engraved much more precisely and legibly on copper. However, the faithful came to realise that Leoni had embellished some of Palladio's elevations with baroque 'improvements', so after several further inadequate versions it was eventually superseded by a faithful one. This was Isaac Ware's of 1738, which was also illustrated by copper engravings and was soon accepted as the definitive edition, which it remains to this day.[6] (John Wood was one of the subscribers.) Ware was the protégé of the wealthy Lord Burlington, who was the collector of almost all Palladio's surviving drawings, a highly gifted amateur architect, and the passionate leader and promoter of the Palladians in Britain. To their twin authorities of Palladio and Vitruvius, they added a third, Inigo Jones, a convinced Palladian who, a century earlier, had introduced classical architecture to Britain. His Palladian influence had been superseded by the baroque of Wren and his school, but was now appreciated again (and theirs inevitably derided). Because the new movement was a return to the principles held by Inigo, Palladianism became the patriotic British style, as opposed to the baroque of the Catholic and absolutist countries on the Continent.

Expensive folios were beyond the means of the craftsmen who were the designers of most buildings. They obtained the necessary knowledge from a flood of cheap pattern books of varying quality. Not all their authors accepted the rule of Palladio enthusiastically, being nostalgic for the days of their youth when imagination was much less constricted. William Halfpenny, for example, a minor architect and author of several pattern books, was critical of Palladio and in one of his books enumerated his 'mistakes' and gave his corrections of them. Another more eminent critic was the painter William Hogarth, who published engravings ridiculing the prevailing orthodoxy and the rule of the five orders. No doubt there were many others whose opinions never reached print.

So the answer to the question, what is Palladianism, is that it was a set of beliefs about the design of architecture which by the 1720s or 30s was held by almost every architect in Britain and by a large number of influential laymen led by Lord Burlington. It was a Rule of Taste in which buildings and their details were either 'correct' if they conformed, or 'incorrect' if they did not. Architects who were incorrect were unlikely to be given commissions.

This was the milieu, and the battlefield, into which the youthful John Wood entered.

6 The quotations from Palladio above were taken from this translation.

4 John Wood

John Wood (1704-1754) was born in Bath, where his father was a minor builder. He attended the local Blue Coat Charity School and his father then apprenticed him to a carpenter and joiner. It isn't known where or to whom he was articled, but since his early contacts were amongst building craftsmen in London, that seems the most probable place. If so it indicates that his father, recognising the limitations of a provincial training in a small country town, had ambitions for his clever son.

In London Wood moved in a loosely knit group of young building tradesmen and materials merchants in the circle around Edward Shepherd, a plasterer who had become one of the leading developers of what we now call the West End. One such contact was James Theobald, a prosperous timber merchant with whom he made an informal arrangement that Theobald would recommend Wood, who in turn would recommend and specify his timber. Somehow Wood must have acquired a small amount of capital, because between 1723 (when he was 19) and 1730 he built five houses in Oxford Street and several others nearby.[1] The capital would have been needed to borrow a larger sum on the security of promised sales. He also appears to have acted as the surveyor for Lord Bingley's large house in Cavendish Square, and as his architect for works at his Bramham Park estate in Yorkshire. What that work was is unknown, but Mowl and Earnshaw in their definitive study of Wood suggested that it was the design and building of the handsome stable block. No doubt he carried out other jobs for Bingley, possibly in the landscaped grounds of which he made an impressive survey published in 1731. In 1727 he returned to Bath and carried out work at the St John's Hospital site for the Duke of Chandos, for whom he had previously worked at Cavendish Square. This job had been previously turned down by Edward Shepherd, who presumably put in a word for him. The Duke proved impossible to please and complained of almost everything. The result was unsatisfactory, which was no doubt due to faults on both sides. John Wood House facing the Cross Bath (14), and Chandos House on the opposite side of the sprawling group of courts and buildings, are the most satisfying bits of Wood's work. Despite the Duke's shrill complaints whilst work was going on, when it was finished he nonetheless recommended Wood to his cousin, William Brydges of Tyberton in Herefordshire, for whom in 1727-8 he carried out alterations to the house and built the sanctuary in the local church.

Whilst he was in Yorkshire Wood heard that Bath Corporation had obtained acts to improve the roads and lighting in and around the city, and the navigability of the 13 miles of Avon down to Bristol. Since changes were clearly imminent, he began to draw up ambitious plans for his native city. Like most architects at that time Wood was passionately interested in Roman

1 To have built several houses at nineteen seems more remarkable now than it did then. The modern prolongation of childhood had not yet started. Seventy three years earlier Wren had become the Gresham Professor of Astronomy at 24, and sixty years later the younger Pitt became Prime Minister at 24, having already served as Chancellor of the Exchequer.

14 John Wood House (the name is modern). Chapel Court front. John Wood, 1727

architecture, but not having been to Italy he knew little more about it than he could discover from his copy of Palladio. Ignorance of such matters was an advantage to him because it gave free rein to his bounding imagination. There was nothing in any of his work so far to suggest that he was going to be anything out of the ordinary, but he was an extraordinary and complex man. Unlike most artisans at that time, many of whom couldn't even write their names, he had received a first-rate classical education at the Blue Coat School. He was thoroughly at home with Latin, and over his short life became extremely erudite, with a wide knowledge of the classical historians and geographers. He wrote several books, including his *Essay Towards a Description of Bath*,[2] all of which are now difficult to read, partly because he was too prolix and his facts so badly organised that useful information pops up unexpectedly, but also because his interminable pages explaining his theories about history, though respectable at the time, are all now known to be incorrect. In the early eighteenth century very little was known about pre-history, except what was written in the Old Testament which was accepted as a literally true history. Some of the greatest minds of the age tried to expand this knowledge. Sir Isaac Newton, and after him Wood, believed that the Pharaoh Sesostris was in fact the Hebrew King Sishak, which made Hebrew civilisation more ancient than the Egyptians', and the Israelites' Tabernacle therefore the first work of architecture. While the young Wood was in London in the 1720s learning by experience about housing development, there was much excited discussion in learned circles about the Tabernacle and Solomon's Temple, and huge entirely speculative models of them were exhibited. Wood came to believe that the Doric, Ionic

2 Published 1742-3. Revised editions in 1749 and 1765. The 1765 edition was reprinted in 1969

and Corinthian orders were revealed by God to the Israelites, and that Vitruvius and others had deliberately falsified history to give their origin to the Greeks. So classical architecture was not merely the most beautiful style, it alone had divine authority. By similar sorts of arguments he and others persuaded themselves that the Druids were Phoenician colonists who brought the religion of Abraham to Britain and built Stonehenge. Wood decided that Bladud, the mythical founder of Bath, was a priest of Apollo and a real historical figure. And so on. It is easy to write off Wood as a crackpot, but in the eighteenth century these now utterly discredited beliefs were very widely accepted. It is extraordinary that this dreamer was also an extremely shrewd and successful business man, an architect of outstanding ability and a town planner of unrivalled genius.

It was well known that Bath had been a Roman town, and when much later in the early 1740s Wood was writing his *Essay*, he quoted the reference to the town by the relatively obscure second-century AD writer Solinus. Wood's return to Bath in 1727 coincided with the discovery of the celebrated gilt bronze head of Minerva. It would not be surprising if a man of Wood's cast of mind felt it to be a portent. He determined to recreate Classical Bath. Since at that time almost nothing was known of it – the Baths, for example, were not discovered until 1755, the year after his death – he was free to imagine the city as he wished.

He proposed to build 'a grand Place of Assembly, to be called the Royal Forum of Bath; another Place, no less magnificent, for the Exhibition of Sports, to be called the Grand Circus, and a third Place, of equal State with either of the former, for the Practice of Medicinal Exercises, to be called the Imperial Gymnasium of the City, from a Work of that kind, taking its Rise at first in Bath, during the Time of the Roman Emperors' (for which there was no evidence whatever). He drew two alternative sets of plans for all this, (unfortunately neither survives) adjusted for entirely separate sites belonging to two different landowners, and sent them off to them. Since it is clear that each of his proposals would have cost a great deal of money and generate very little, inevitably he was going to be disappointed. It is the only indication that despite all his experience and reading this 20-year-old was still not much more than a boy. But he soon learnt the financial lesson whilst never abandoning the essence of the dream. In an extraordinary way he and his son between them eventually built almost all of it.

After his return to Bath Wood soon faced up to the fact that his ambitious plans were not going to be accepted by either of the landowners or anybody else. In London he had learnt to design competently in the Palladian manner; he knew how the speculative housing market and its complicated finances worked; how the aristocratic London estates were being developed on an orderly plan prepared for the landowner, and erected by a variety of speculating builders who had to conform to it. More slowly, and at some cost to his clients, such as the Duke of Chandos, he had learnt how to build within the constraints of time and budget. He could see, better than anybody in Bath, that the squires and aristocrats whom Beau Nash was increasingly attracting to the city could not find lodgings equal to what he and his

15 Queen Square, north
side. John Wood, 1736

associates were building for them in London. There was a gap in the market. He made his name with Queen Square. (15) Historians have always recognised its importance, but have not acknowledged that in designing it he faced an entirely new problem. The squares which had made any sort of splash up to that time, whether at Peckwater Quad in Oxford, at Covent Garden and the West End in London, or at Queen Square in Bristol, had all been built on *flat* sites. The essential problem of urban development in Georgian Bath was that much of it had to take place on the slopes of Lansdown Hill. As hundreds of subsequent designers throughout the world have discovered, it is extremely difficult to design a square, or any other large geometrical space, which will make its point properly on a slope. To this day Queen Square is one of the few instances where it has been done with complete success. Initially Wood considered levelling the ground, but he sensibly rejected it because all the techniques of levelling a site are expensive, and in Queen Square, he tells us, would have cost £4,000 (around £375,000 today[3]). Wood had not enough capital to borrow that. Everything had to be borrowed on the security of the leases.

3 Based on Evelyn Smith, who in his table *Historical Value of money in the UK*, gives a multiplier of 94.1 for 1730. His data relate to September 1997. Although they themselves are now out of date, I use them throughout this book.

As we shall see later in chapter 6, in the eighteenth and early nineteenth centuries it was not uncommon for builders to create level platforms for their developments, either by raising the ground level artificially on vaults, or by a mixture of cut and fill. But this was very dangerous. Money spent at the beginning of a project on such site works is much more expensive than the same sum spent near the end, because the period of the loan is longer and the accumulated interest, always high for speculative projects of this sort, correspondingly higher. When levelling operations of this type cover a large area they become hugely expensive and were such a burden on a development that many speculating builders who undertook them went bankrupt. Wood knew that: he had to design himself out of the problem.

On a square built across a slope, the uphill and downhill sides will be level and only the two sides will have to slope. Wood realised that if he could create a sufficiently powerful design on the uphill, north, side of Queen Square, he could make the two sloping sides so secondary a part of the concept that the interruption of their symmetry by the slope would be of little importance. He took advantage of the fact that the ground sloped down to the south. This meant that his dominant terrace of houses on the uphill side of the square would face the sun and thus be the most attractive to purchasers. In his *Essay* he said that his design for it was intended 'to group ordinary town houses in such a way as to gain the effect of a single palace', words to be repeated or paraphrased by countless writers ever since. (15) The Square was completed in 1736, eight years after it was planned.

The land belonged to Robert Gay, a surgeon living in London. Wood leased a total of about five acres, taking a little at a time over a period from November 1728 to October 1734. Each of the seven leases was for a period of 99 years. On each occasion he divided the piece he had just leased into house plots, and sublet them on 98-year leases to carpenters, masons, plumbers and other craftsmen who would build them speculatively. They had relative freedom internally and at the back,[4] but were required to build the façade Wood had designed, and could use their lease as security to borrow the necessary money. When Wood had let all the sub-leases on a piece of land his annual income from them was greater than his rent to Gay, so he could lease another piece, for which he would previously have prepared a design. When the Square and the adjacent land was finally complete, Wood was paying Gay £137 per annum, but receiving £305 from his sub-leases, an annual profit of £168, around £15,000 today. It was a respectable regular income (fixed for 90 odd years!) for a young man who must have been almost penniless a few years before. He could use this fixed income as collateral if he needed to.

His role involved a great deal more than merely preparing the design and arranging the sub-leases. The whole organisation was an extremely formidable problem because, to take the example of the north side of Queen Square, it wasn't possible for each team member to build his own vertical strip of façade without it being horribly apparent in the finished work. The entire façade could only be built successfully by one mason and his team. Calculating his and the other members' financial contributions, and the constant resolution of problems arising between team members and the junctions of their spheres of work, required a very high degree of technical knowledge and leadership from Wood.

He started by building round the corner in what is now Wood Street, before beginning on the sloping east side of the Square. (16) This side is a terrace of six houses, the two end ones having

4 Frank Lloyd Wright, who disliked classical architecture, on his only visit to Britain was taken to Bath. He was not impressed. He said the houses were Queen Anne before and Mary Anne behind.

16 Queen Square, east side

only narrow frontages onto the Square and their main fronts around the two corners. The next houses in, the second and fifth in the row, project a few inches forward from the others, providing an articulation which is not very apparent on the ground, largely because the terrace steps up at the points where it projects forward, and the vertical steps are more marked than the horizontal ones. This organisation of the façade is respectable and works well enough, but, as Wood intended, it doesn't draw attention to itself. When leases of these houses had been taken he screwed up his courage and began on the much more attention-grabbing north side of the Square.

It was a dangerous venture for two main reasons. The first was the simple fact that its architectural elaboration made the houses much more expensive than all the others so far, and thus the craftsmen who had to take Wood's leases, and the people whom they had to persuade to lend them the necessary finance, were all going to be more nervous of agreeing to do so unless they were certain there would be a taker for each house. That was a longish chain of people to be persuaded, and it had to be in place for every plot. The second reason why the speculation was dangerous grew out of the first. Initial purchasers of speculatively built houses always worry – or they should – that not all the houses or plots will be taken, and they will have to live, or try to persuade a tenant to live, on a muddy uncompleted estate or in a half-built terrace. That is bad enough, but on the north side of Queen Square they could have ended up living in a terrace with half a pediment, or no matching pavilion at one end. Wood probably knew that this was about to happen in London, where his colleague Edward Shepherd was building a somewhat similar pedimented terrace in Grosvenor Square, but had discovered too late that he couldn't get enough land to finish it. For Wood, something of that sort happening to him would have been a constant nightmare. It never did, he was far too competent a business man.

In fact things did get very sticky because the demand for leases throughout the whole Square went slowly. Comfortably off people in Bath were accustomed to houses asserting their individuality, like Rosewell House then nearing completion, and were probably still not comfortable with the idea of living in a terrace in which their house would be only an anonymous part. To speed them up Wood followed the Earl of Bedford's precedent in Covent Garden and built a (now lost) church to serve the Square, just outside but facing into

17 St Mary's Chapel. John Wood, 1734, demolished c.1875. From Mowbray Green

it at the south-west corner. (17) But he turned the idea up a notch and made it proprietary. A proprietary chapel was one built as a speculation by an individual or, as in this instance, a group of shareholders. Their return came from several sources: leasing the benefice to a clergyman; the sale or rent of the pews; and the sale of burial vaults in the basement, of which St Mary's Chapel as Wood named it, had 27. (It was called a chapel because, although Anglican, it was not a parish church but built in an existing parish.) Building began in 1732 and the Chapel was consecrated by the bishop two years later. Its investment value was an incidental advantage: its great value to Wood was that it gave reassurance to potential house purchasers. In the eighteenth century the availability of pews in a nearby fashionable church had exactly the same effect on house lettings as the availability of car parking on office lettings today. As Wood triumphantly records in his *Essay*, the Chapel had the desired effect and produced 17 new takers for houses in the Square, including enough to complete the north side. What he didn't record was that he then sold his share in the Chapel at a profit.

On Fourdrinier's engraving of the north side of the Square, (18) which is one of the illustrations in his *Essay*, Wood says he designed it in 1728, which is when he took his first leases from Gay. That was probably the year when Shepherd began building his side of Grosvenor Square in London, which suggests that he had designed it a year or two earlier. So although all the dates are too uncertain to be sure, it seems that Shepherd produced his elevation before Wood drew his. Wood had presumably seen Shepherd's design, but although he followed its general idea his design was decisively different and much richer.

In some ways it was quite close to Dean Aldrich's elevations at Peckwater Quad in Oxford, because they both had pediments and both were hexastyle (six columned). It is highly doubtful whether Wood knew it because it wasn't illustrated in *Vitruvius Britannicus*, and it isn't very likely that he had ever been to Oxford. Whether he knew it or not, his highly professional design is distinctly superior to Aldrich's clever but amateur performance.

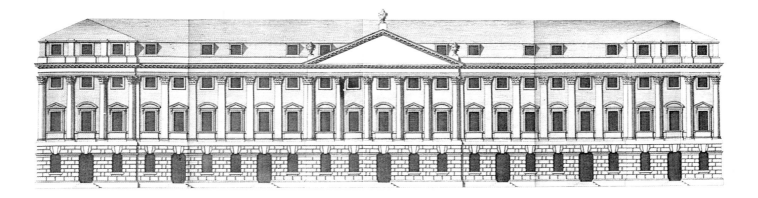

At Peckwater the three sides are continuous, with no gap between them. In Queen Square the sides are separated from each other by a road. The junctions between the sides defeated Aldrich, who made a mess of them. Wood's building is more plastic or three-dimensional, and his Square builds up to a marvellous climax on the north side, whilst Aldrich's repetitive sides are consequently duller. Comparison of the details is equally revealing. The ground-floor rustication in Wood's version, for example, is given greater emphasis by being extended below the window cills, instead of starting at that level as in Aldrich's; and Wood's omission of the flat frames or architraves around the ground-floor window and door openings, which so confuse the rustication pattern on Aldrich's Quad, gives much greater clarity to his basic idea. It was a masterly piece of work, clearly superior to anything of the sort built in England previously. Quite rightly it made Wood's name.

The original design of the Square's sloping west side matched the one opposite, but this had to be scrapped because the mansion of a recalcitrant leaseholder who refused to budge was set back behind a forecourt in the centre of the projected terrace. So, instead of a unified terrace stepping house by house up the slope, Wood designed two conventional but very beautiful Palladian blocks, one at the top and the other at the bottom of the slope, each with a rusticated basement taking up the fall in the ground, and with plain ashlar upper storeys. Because they were separated by a wide gap their difference in level from each other didn't matter. Set back between them was the mansion. (19) The result was brilliant, probably better than Wood's initial design, and far better than what we see today because a century later, in 1830, the gap was filled by three more houses designed by the younger John Pinch. Considered on their own they have considerable interest and beauty, but here they are an ugly disaster because they are so deeply unsympathetic to Wood's work, destroying the harmony of the whole side. Their heavy entablature, for example, draws attention to the discrepancy in level of Wood's two pavilions. Long before the 1830s, buildings of the early Georgian period had come to be seen as hopelessly dull and old-fashioned, and their alteration or destruction matters of no concern. (See chapter 7 for an analysis of Pinch's design.)

Today Queen Square is a deeply unpleasant traffic roundabout, ruined by the vehicles on the London Road passing through it. Originally the enclosing roads were narrower, the pavements wider, the houses occupied by families and not businesses, and the formal planting in the central garden was much more sympathetic. The damage inflicted by the wartime bombing of Bath has all been put right, the damage inflicted by the subsequent growth of traffic worsens. Queen Square is today the most damaged part of Classical Bath.

WEST SIDE OF QUEEN SQUARE AS ORIGINALLY DESIGNED.

19 West side of Queen Square as it was originally. Sketch by Mowbray Green

At some time in the 1730s Wood designed a house with a very rich façade in Chippenham's High Street. It introduced one of Wood's favourite motifs when the budget was large enough to afford it, masks and swags running between the Corinthian capitals. A few years later he was to use them on a much extended version of this front on his superlative Exchange in Bristol. During the 1920s and 1930s Chippenham's once delightful High Street was ruined as house after house was demolished or altered to make way for modern shops. It provided one of the classic horror stories cited then and later in the campaign to prevent that sort of thing happening again. One of the early protesters was a wealthy Bath resident, Ernest Cook, grandson of the travel agent Thomas Cook. He bought the façade in 1936, just before Woolworths knocked it down, and re-erected it to form the side elevation of his end terrace house in Sion Hill Place. It is now a part of Kingswood Prep School and can be seen only from its private grounds. (20) In fact the façade doesn't look entirely satisfactory in its new location. It was designed by Wood to be one of a continuous tight line of varied façades. Here, standing alone with plenty of space on either side, it looks hunched-up, its windows and pilasters squeezed too tightly together. In its original setting it would have looked much better. Nonetheless it is a splendid façade and all praise to Ernest Cook for having saved it. (It was he who five years earlier had bought the fast deteriorating Upper Assembly Rooms and given them to the National Trust.[5])

In his books Wood comes over as a cranky, bookish, man, jealous of rivals and anxious to do them down, probably without much charm or ease with his social superiors. For whatever reason, he wasn't able to build a lucrative practice designing great aristocratic houses, as other

---

5 There is a legend, which most scholars appear to take seriously, that the house was originally built by Wood at Bowden Hill in Wiltshire, then demolished and rebuilt at Chippenham. I am sceptical. In the 18th century it was almost unknown to move a building or even a façade in this way, though there were a few rare instances of small structures, such as Inigo Jones's gateway which Lord Burlington moved to Chiswick from Beaufort House in Chelsea. That there should have been two resurrections of Wood's façade stretches credulity almost to breaking point, even ignoring the fact that its design is appropriate for a street but not for a country house.

20 Façade moved from Chippenham High Street in 1936. It now forms the west front of the end house in Sion Hill Place.
John Wood, 1730s

provincial architects such as Carr of York or Smith of Warwick were able to do. So it is not entirely surprising that although he was given several commissions in and around Bath, most of his important buildings in the city were the result of his own enterprise or of you-scratch-my-back-and-I'll-scratch-yours trade connections. The most important of these was his relationship with Ralph Allen. Allen had made a great fortune from the nation-wide postal system he had set up and ran from his house in Liliput Alley, but he then saw untapped financial potential in Bath stone. He therefore bought the two quarries on Combe Down which produced it, and like successful but ruthless entrepreneurs in all periods, scrapped the inefficient old ways, built a horse-drawn railway to carry the stone from the quarries down to his quay in central Bath, sacked the masons and carters who resisted change, and employed Wood to bring more adaptable and up-to-date masons down from Yorkshire. In about 1737 Wood then built him two splendid rows of cottages to house them, one adjacent to the quarry and one beside the quay. (21)

He next employed Wood to extend his house in Liliput Alley. Wood's authorship has been questioned, but in his *Essay* he says quite clearly that 'the Designs, as well as the Model for this Addition, were made while I was in London', they are 'a sample of the greatest magnificence that was ever proposed by me for our city houses'. (His even richer Circus was still in the future.) Wood's work consisted of a central range with side wings projecting from it to enclose a garden enjoying views over Claverton Down, which Allen soon improved in the fashionable

21 Ralph Allen Cottages. John Wood, 1737

22 Ralph Allen's town-house. John Wood, 1727

manner by the erection of a Sham Castle on the hill top. After Allen moved to Prior Park, the house continued to accommodate his postal business, but one of the side wings and part of the other were demolished and the garden filled with houses, leaving only the central feature of the central range untouched. Enthusiasts can still see it, or some of it, squeezed between houses off North Parade Passage. (22) Remembering that it is only a fragment, I have always found it enchanting, unlike most previous writers who have carped at it. The young Wood was playing what Lutyens called the Great Game, using well established classical motifs in new combinations and forms. The narrow façade is basically the familiar four Corinthian columns standing on a rusticated basement and supporting a pediment, in this case filled with glorious swirling ornament. Playing behind the four columns he introduced another familiar Palladian motif, a Venetian window, but here spread out so that the wide-arched central element occupies the whole of the central bay, and the two flat-topped elements occupy the narrower side bays. Who else was there in the west of England who could have made something so ingenious and so lovely?

But a modest town house wasn't enough for Allen. He was becoming very rich and wanted the world to know it, and he wanted to show that his stone was not only suitable for houses, but for palaces as well. He decided to employ Wood to build one for him on a dream site at the head of a valley to the south of the city. The early history of Prior Park is not fully known, and what is known is horribly confused, despite Mowl and Earnshaw's comprehensive research. It appears that the design, based on an engraving of an unbuilt house by Colen Campbell in the first volume of his *Vitruvius Britannicus*, was forced on Wood. Wood, who, though still little known outside Bath, was a better designer than Campbell, can't have been happy about that. Even so, his design

23 Prior Park, north façade.
John Wood, 1741.
The steps up to the
house are possibly by
H.E. Goodridge, c.1820s

was distinctly superior to Campbell's, being taller, shorter and with a more boldly projecting portico. (23) The long low wings, which were canted forward to follow the contours, were, Wood wrote in his *Essay*, designed to form three sides of an imaginary duodecagon three quarters of a mile in diameter. That was an inflated way of saying that each wing was designed at an angle of 120° to the house. If things started unhappily they soon got worse because Allen kept changing his mind. Work started on the west wing, into which Allen moved in 1735. In 1741 he was able to move into the central block, but before that, when only its lower storey had been built, Wood, who by then was becoming known nationally, had had enough and resigned, to be replaced by his untalented but more biddable Clerk of Works, Richard Jones. The chief causes of the trouble were Jones's alterations to the west wing which Allen had instructed him to make without consulting Wood, and Allen's decision to have his main entrance on the uphill, south, side of the house, when everything had been designed for it to be entered through the great half-built portico on the north side, facing downhill towards Bath. It has to be admitted that Wood's proposal to enter on the north was foolish because it would have meant climbing 30 steps up to the entrance, whereas entry on the uphill side would have required only a few. The reason of course was that on this side of the house facing the city, Wood was going all out for magnificence, to which Allen agreed until, far too late, he realised the consequence. Wood should have known better: back at the design stage he should have discussed the issue very fully with Allen, pointing out the disadvantage as well as the benefit. The change made a nonsense of his planning, and the necessary alterations would inevitably be a botch. Jones stumbled on, building a symmetrical east wing and finishing as near to Wood's design as possible.

Apart from that, the differences between what was built and what Wood intended were not very great. He later published in his *Essay* an engraving of the main elevation of the central block 'with the windows dressed according to the original design'. At the lower level their alternately segmental and triangular pediments were supported by Corinthian columns instead of the cheaper architraves which were actually built, and at the upper level the entablatures were omitted from the framing architraves. These would have been heart-breaking for Wood but are of little consequence except in very close views.

The façade does have a slight awkwardness for which Wood alone was responsible. British architects, unlike some seventeenth-century Italian ones, have usually preferred to design their façades with a length of wall at each end which is identical to, or slightly wider than the interval between window and window. Palladio advised that 'the windows, and other openings, ought to be as far distant from the angles as possible; or at least so much space must be left between the aperture and the angles as the width of the opening or void.' At Prior Park Wood chose the minimum allowed by Palladio (anything less would be a structural weakness). To English eyes at least, it makes the façade look as though it has been truncated at each end. Fortunately it doesn't matter in the distant views which most people enjoy. What does matter is the glorious hexastyle portico and its pediment standing so boldly out from the wall. It may not be as Wood intended, but when looked at from the town or from the bottom of the valley, the damaged side wings are almost out of sight and of little significance. (see frontispiece) The exterior of the central block towering on its hilltop as he intended, is glorious: something of which, despite the pinpricks he had suffered along the way, he was rightly proud.

24 Prior Park Chapel, apse, now without its altar and altarpiece. John Wood 1741. The Chapel is the only interior by Wood to survive in the house

The main block of the house has been twice devastated by fire, on both occasions only the chapel being unaffected. There, apart from the loss of the painted altar piece and the coved flat ceiling which has been replaced by a featureless plaster barrel vault, everything remains in very good condition. It's a curious and unsettling space because it's too tall for its small size. That apart, the chapel is superb. There is an apse at the east end (24) and a gallery at the west. The north wall contains at high level a Venetian window, and reflecting it on the south wall, a matching organ gallery, now without its organ. The lower walls are Ionic and the upper Corinthian. Wood's ample budget allowed him to give the walls great three-dimensional richness, with huge surging flows of mouldings in the entablatures. None of his other buildings,

25 Prior Park Chapel.
Entablature and
plaster vaulting over
the west gallery

THE CLASSICAL BUILDINGS OF BATH

before and after this one, reveal so clearly his deep, almost passionate love of this classical apparatus. The whole of the interior is now painted, which certainly is not what he intended, and the modern colour scheme, white and very pale cream, is not something he would have admired, but it has the enormous merit of allowing the purity of his mouldings to shine out with absolute clarity. Wood was in his early 30s when he designed this chapel, with very little experience of designing large formal interiors. They are much more difficult to design than exteriors because no drawings can adequately convey the sense of space: mastery of that comes only after built trial and error, and it must explain the awkward proportion of the space here. Wood had never been to Italy; had never stood inside Palladio's San Georgio Maggiore or the Redentore, which could have taught him so much. The wonder is that at his first major attempt he came so close. However, the projection in and out of the features enlivening his walls is superb, and on the gallery his wonderful mastery of the flow of the entablature's mouldings is beyond praise. (25)

In 1755 the views up to the house and down from it were greatly improved when Allen instructed Jones to dam the little stream which runs intermittently down the valley to form a small lake, and to build across it a copy of the glorious Palladian Bridge at Wilton. (26 and frontispiece) Despite its name this most lovely and imitated of all garden buildings was not designed by Palladio, though it incorporates several of his ideas for bridges. Its conception was Lord Pembroke's, to make a loggia for alfresco tea parties over the river Nadder in his park at Wilton, and its 1737 execution and detailed architectural treatment was the work of his architect Roger Morris. No sooner was it complete than the Earl's fellow Whig, Lord Cobham, built a close imitation in his estate at Stowe. This was followed in 1759 by Allen's version at Prior Park, and in 1764 by another at Hagley. Many years ago, in my ignorance I was astonished to find yet another, in Catherine the Great's garden at Tsarskoe Selo near St Petersburg. (Like all the superb palaces and churches at Leningrad, as it was then called, it had been impeccably restored by the Stalinist government after the devastating bombardment during the city's Siege. It put to shame our puny efforts at rebuilding, and our readiness to destroy what the bombing had spared.)

The Bridge wasn't the end of the story at Prior Park, because in 1829 the Roman Catholic Bishop Baines bought what had by then become a huge white elephant, and converted it into a seminary, adding a storey to the east wing. Then there was the devastating fire of 1836. Baines's reconstruction was destructive of Wood's work, but it was another example of the inevitable reaction of one generation against the work of its immediate predecessors. After

---

6 Baines was a great one for depending on the Lord to provide, which He frequently declined to do. The seminary proved to be uneconomic and after Baines's death had to close. Eventually the whole building was re-opened as the Roman Catholic grammar school which it remains to this day, now co-educational. In Bristol the bishop commenced an enormous pro-cathedral that was so beyond the church's means that, when only a hugely expensive platform and a few giant columns had been built, work stopped, never to resume. A cheap gothic church was later built on the platform, where it has lain idle ever since 1973 when a new cathedral was built in Clifton.

26 Prior Park, Palladian Bridge, 1755. Copy by Richard Jones of Lord Pembroke's 1737 original at Wilton, for which the executive architect was Roger Morris

the death of Bishop Baines[6] the Catholics did create one outstanding building within the complex, a church in the west wing begun by the Roman Catholic J. J. Scoles in 1844, but not completed until after his death by one of his sons. It is too important to be described out of chronological sequence here, so that must wait. Also of that late period are the gloriously swirling baroque steps climbing the last few metres up to the great north portico that was in fact Allen's back door.

Two or three years before he completed Queen Square, Wood received a commission for a small country house from Francis Yerbury, one of the more successful woolen manufacturers of Bradford-on-Avon, who exported his superfine cloth as far as Turkey, where, he claimed, it was particularly popular with the ladies of the Sultan's Seraglio. Wood completed the house, Belcombe Brook, in 1734. The budget was obviously tight because only the garden front was faced with ashlar. Wood told the readers of his *Essay* that his Ionic pilastered front was 'the best tetrastyle frontispiece in square pillars that hath yet been executed in or about Bath. The windows of the principal storey are dressed so as to become complete tabernacles, while those of the half storey are adorned with single architraves.' The parlour is 20 feet square, and the

12-foot octagonal study, one of Wood's best surviving domestic interiors, has a coved ceiling, the flat portion of which has plasterwork 'performed by a workman of great skill'.

Many years later, in 1748, the by then famous Wood designed another small country house near Bath, Titanbarrow Loggia. He was obviously fond of tall rooms with coved ceilings, following Palladio's rule that the height of a room should be the same as its width. That was fine in a hot country but very uncomfortable in a colder one. In a large country house with a profusion of rooms of all sizes that didn't matter, in winter the noble occupants could use the more comfortable smaller ones. But at Titanbarrow there was only one drawing room. It occupied the three bays of the show front and rose the full height of the house. Eventually the owner lowered the ceiling and built some new rooms above it. In order to do this a range of first-floor windows had to be cut into the façade. The work was done sympathetically and the result is far from disastrous, but the façade is too crowded and no longer Wood's.

At some date in the late 1730s or early 1740s Wood designed, though sensibly only in outline, his most ambitious and unrealistic plan. It was for an enormous Forum, over a thousand feet long and ringed by 340 columns. The canalised Avon would flow through bridges on either side of it into a great octagonal basin which, he had no doubt, would fill with ships, just like one of Claude's harbour scenes. Wood claimed in the 1742 edition of his *Essay* that building would start in the following year. Of course it didn't and never could. The cost would have been gigantic and the practical benefit slight. But what a dream! Only a pope or a Continental monarch could have built such a thing as a memorial of his greatness, and in Britain we have no tradition of that, with only the Prince Regent and his architect John Nash as a later and partial exception. When Wood began to sense the reality of the situation he trimmed his design down, but even then it was never to be.

In fact a small preliminary part of it was built and survives, the North and South Parades, which were designed to look over the Forum. When it was clear that the several, increasingly reduced, versions of the Forum were never going to be built, in 1738 Wood went ahead with the Parades. He designed them as rows of individual houses treated, like Queen Square, as unified palaces. (27) As he had done in Queen Square, he let out leases for the individual houses, most of them being taken up by the craftsmen who would build them. This time the enterprise was going to be more expensive than the earlier version because it had to be raised on a high platform, the front of which is 18 feet above ground. Some of the leaseholders rebelled, probably led by Ralph Allen who had taken one or two as a speculation: profit was always more important to him than architectural distinction. Wood had to cut out his proposed Corinthian columns and was even forced to build the terrace wall in rubble stonework instead of the more urbane ashlar. Since then further changes have whittled away much of the development's character. Even so, the Parades and their wide pavements are still impressive, but they could have been designed by anybody: they show none of Wood's genius. It was to be several years before he ventured into the field of housing in Bath again.

27 South Parade.
John Wood, 1738

In 1742 he was asked to design new premises for the ancient King Edward's Grammar School. After he and the Corporation disagreed about the site, Thomas Jelly was appointed. His building, on a new site in Broad Street, was opened in 1752 – designed in an excellent version of Wood's style of 25 years earlier. (28)

Visitors to Bath had spread Wood's reputation throughout the country, which obtained him commissions to design the Exchanges of Bristol and Liverpool. The superlative Bristol building of 1741-3, which alone of the two survives externally in good order, has a façade which is a variation on the theme of the Queen Square façade, but shorter and – with a much bigger budget – tightened up to a higher degree of intensity.[7] It has always been recognised as the best post-medieval building in Bristol. In 1749 Wood was commissioned to design the Exchange at Liverpool, now much altered and converted to use as the Town Hall.

Way back in the 1720s a group of Bath citizens had formed a charity to collect money to build a hospital utilising the healing waters. Their Treasurer was the apothecary Humphrey Thayer, who commissioned the young Wood, then still working in London, to acquire a suitable site near the King's Bath and prepare a plan. Mowl and Earnshaw suggest that this was what Wood, with typical grandiosity, had proposed as an Imperial Gymnasium. After many false starts the present constricted site was acquired in 1738 and what is now called the Royal National Hospital for Rheumatic Diseases was built to Wood's design, opening in 1741. (29) Wood, who was by

7 I compare the two elevations in *An architectural history of Bristol*, Gomme and Jenner, 2011

28 King Edward's
Grammar School.
Thomas Jelly, 1752

then one of Bath's leading citizens, had given his services free of charge and was elected as one of the Governors. It is difficult to judge the façade fairly today because when early-eighteenth-century Palladian design was out of fashion and despised, an attic storey was added in the late 1790s and the whole façade extended in the 1850s. Furthermore, it faces north and rarely benefits from Bath stone's glorious glow when the sun shines on it. The result is that people who pass it every day seldom look at it, and nobody has felt called upon to raise the money to replace the glazing bars in the windows. However, if one looks at the photograph of the façade and covers the top storey with a piece of paper, it is fascinating to see how greatly the proportions improve. The façade, with its pedimented Ionic tetrastyle central pavilion, is a splendid piece of work.

If Wood had died after finishing these buildings he would be known as one of the better English

29 The Royal National Hospital for Rheumatic Diseases. John Wood 1738-41. Attic storey added by John Palmer, 1792

Palladian architects. But he didn't die, and he hadn't yet displayed the full force of his genius, the design of a sequence of streets: what we now call urban design. There he was not one of several near equals, he was the greatest this country has produced.

In the 1750s he returned to the design of housing in Bath, this time with a partner, his son John the younger (1728-1781), who had been conceived in the year before his father conceived the elevation for the north side of Queen Square. Wood had taken the central house in the Square's south side, so that every day he could enjoy looking at the opposite side, his finest achievement in Bath so far. From his windows he could also see the respectable but routine houses he then began developing in Barton Street (which he later renamed Gay Street) going up the hill to Gay's Fields beyond. At that time they and some precipitous land on the London Road were the only available sites in Bath suitable for large-scale house building,[8] so Gay Street was the key to the only land for which Wood could obtain leases.

Most of the houses in Gay Street follow the general pattern he had established for the east side of Queen Square, but two of them, designed for specific rather than potential occupiers, are individually designed. No. 41, the bow-fronted house on the corner at the bottom, was commissioned by a rich Quaker. (30) Wood designed it so that its main rooms on each floor are set diagonally into the house, and face diagonally into the Square. He designed these three rooms with a semi-circular bow at front and back, making them, in effect, oval in shape. Unlike many of his French contemporaries, Wood never designed his house plans with a variety of

8 There was plenty of flat land at Bathwick, but it was inaccessible, being cut off by the river until the building of Pulteney Bridge made it available. See chapter 6.

circular, oval and rectangular rooms. In this case he came close to it. Externally, he made the bow's fenestration emphatic to draw attention to the junction between Queen Square and Gay Street. The ground-floor windows have Gibbs surrounds, those on the first floor have heavily blocked pairs of Ionic columns, the centre one being arched. The most fascinating detail of all is the heavy cornice above these first-floor windows, which appears to terminate the bow, except that it continues up to the parapet so that the second-floor windows are more like attic windows. Everything is logical and 'correct'; there is nothing either baroque or rococo about it as some writers have claimed. The interiors are splendid, the beautiful drawing room on the first floor being particularly interesting because the apse is framed by Corinthian columns on pedestals. (31) In grand houses at this time it was quite common for the walls of the larger rooms to be articulated by columns in this way, but being expensive and space consuming they were rare in more modest town houses, where instead the wall was ordered as though they were present. There the dado was the equivalent of the pedestal, and the height of the wall above was equivalent to the column and its capital. Above were the entablature and cornice, or sometimes the frieze and cornice alone.

The other Gay Street house with an elaborated façade is No. 8, commissioned by the sculptor Prince Hoare.[9] (32) The three windows on each floor are grouped more tightly together than those in the adjoining houses. At ground level they are linked by an entablature supported on Corinthian pilasters, and on the first floor by an entablature which breaks forward over the central windows to support a pediment. Later in the century Mrs Thrale lived here, and in the mid-twentieth century the house was owned by Dame Edith Sitwell.

A couple of hundred metres after leaving Queen Square, Gay Street comes to a flatter area on which Wood planned a road junction to give access to the development land on its east and west. The obvious thing to do was plan a further sequence of squares and streets, which is what had been happening to everybody's satisfaction in London for most of the last hundred years. But Wood was still driven by his youthful plan for a magnificent *place* 'for the Exhibition of Sports, to be

30 Number 41 Gay Street. John Wood, 1736

31 Drawing room at no.41

9 Prince Hoare's nobility was like Duke Ellington's and Count Basie's

32 Number 8 Gay Street.
John Wood, c.1740

called the Grand Circus'. In mid-eighteenth century Bath the only popular sports were not suitable for public exhibition, but Wood saw a marvellous opportunity to build a Circus of houses. The original Circus in Rome was a long rectangular arena with one rounded end, but it was not this he was thinking of but the Colosseum, which is elliptical. His three-legged road junction logically suggested a circle, which was supported by his almost fanatical interest in the Druids and their stone circles of Stanton Drew and Stonehenge, as well as by the Italian renaissance belief that the circle was the ideal shape. So, maybe without the need for much conscious thought, he introduced into Britain what was to be one of the permanent repertoire of shapes for the urban designer, and gave the word circus its modern meaning of a circular *place*.[10]

Although the circular *place* had not been seen in Britain before,[11] in France at that precise time it was in the thoughts and on the drawing boards of most of the leading architects. French kings (and presidents) have always taken more initiative in architecture and city planning than British ones. In England, with the sole exception of the Prince Regent's great works in London, all the really notable achievements have been carried through by private individuals. Europe's first circular urban space was probably the Place des Victoires in Paris, designed by Jules Hardouin Mansart and built in about 1685. In 1748, when Wood must have been making the first sketches for his Circus, Louis XV held a competition to plan a suitable setting for his equestrian statue by Bouchardon. At least seven of the *places* proposed were circular, though the eventual winner, now called the Place de la Concorde, was not. It isn't possible to say whether Wood knew of the Place des Victoires or of the recent competition. It seems rather a coincidence if he did not, but in the arts what zoologists call convergent evolution is fairly common.

10 The English language is deficient in this respect. We have no words to describe an open urban space unless it is square or circular. I therefore use the French word *place*, which means an urban space of any shape, but I have to put it into italics to make my meaning clear.

11 Inigo Jones had designed a circular court for the abortive Palace of Westminster.

Wood obviously realised that his design would be meaningless unless the site was made entirely flat, because here every house was to have equal emphasis, with no dominating element such as the uphill north side of Queen Square. By this time he was more financially secure, so he was able to start proceedings by levelling the ground. (Examination of the contours on a modern map suggests that the problem was easier than it would have been in Queen Square.) He leased the land from Gay, and sub-leased plots to builders who had to adhere rigidly to the design of his façade, but could do what they liked behind it. This time, however, his design for the façade was far more elaborate and expensive than any row of houses built in Britain before.

The three roads that enter the Circus divide the surrounding façade into three equal segments. Each is identical in design, and un-Palladian in having no points of emphasis, no central or end pavilions. The reason is clearly that Wood thought of the Circus as a continuous circle, not as three separate buildings. This continuity is very strongly emphasised by the powerful horizontal lines of the entablatures at each floor level. The horizontality is almost as powerfully matched by the verticality produced by the pairs of columns between each window. If one uses the

33 The Circus. Designed by John Wood in about 1748 and built by his son, 1755-67

34 The Circus, lower floors. The iron balconettes were added later, probably in about 1800

draughtsman's old trick of looking at it with one eye shut and the other half closed (which cuts out the incidentals and reveals the underlying form) the façade is seen as a simple grid repeated endlessly around the circle. (33) This lack of any variety in intensity as one goes around the circle is paralleled by a similar lack of emphasis vertically, between one storey and another, which is also un-Palladian. The ground floor is in the Roman Doric order, with coupled three-quarter columns supporting an entablature with its correct triglyphs and metopes in the frieze. (34) There is no rustication, only the elaboration of its frieze makes this level slightly heavier than the upper storeys. The three orders are used in their 'correct' Vitruvian sequence, with Doric on the ground floor, Ionic on the first and Corinthian on the top. Visually the top floor is almost as heavy as the bottom one because Wood employed an enriched version of the motif he had first used at Chippenham and then at Bristol, a band of carved ornament running between the capitals of the Corinthian columns. (He took the idea from Inigo Jones's Banqueting House in Whitehall, who took it from Palladio's Palazzo Porto-Braganza.) Because each storey has its own entablature there is no crowning cornice in scale with the whole façade. Wood coped with this common and sometimes unsolved problem by capping the façade with a solid parapet (again un-Palladian), which serves the same function visually. Over each pair of columns he placed not a meaningless urn or vase, but a huge Druidic – and indisputably British – acorn. (The oval holes in the parapet were cut later to allow the servants living in the attics a little more light and view: an ingenious and attractive solution.) Where the three streets come into the Circus, Wood had to solve a difficult problem – how to resolve the junctions between their simple elevations and his highly elaborate Circus elevation. The standard eighteenth-century solution was to return the more elaborate façade around the corner for a few bays, thus giving it an appearance of three-dimensional solidity. Wood rejected this, almost certainly because of its cost, and designed a simplified version in which only the three cornices of his orders turn the corner and run across the flank walls. When looked at from inside the Circus the entablatures terminate over the last pair of columns, set back a few inches, and the cornices alone then continue across a couple of feet of blank wall before turning the corners into the side streets. (36) This is an extremely attractive and neat arrangement, which by omitting to return the highly expensive façade onto the six flank walls saved a lot of money, but it means that the elaborate Circus elevation is treated more like a membrane stretched across the façades than

35 The Circus.
An entrance hall

as a three-dimensional construction which reveals its solidity by returning at the corners. The contradiction between its real solidity and its membrane-like treatment is the sort of ambiguity enjoyed by architects today, but not by many academic architects or critics in the eighteenth or nineteenth centuries. Nor would they have appreciated Wood's several departures from Palladian, and sometimes classical orthodoxy, though we can enjoy them.

36 Return of the Circus
into Gay Street

Few people have ever doubted Wood's brilliance as an urban planner, but opinions on the Circus's purely architectural merit have always differed, probably with a preponderance of criticism over praise. This response is understandable, even if one doesn't share it. Of all the styles of architecture English Palladianism comes nearest to being a series of variations on a limited number of themes, most of them laid down by Palladio and a few other architects such as Serlio and Scamozzi, and then selected by Inigo Jones and Lord Burlington. To put it brutally, in Britain Palladian buildings were expected to look very much like other Palladian buildings. The north side of Queen Square does: the Circus doesn't. In fact it doesn't look like *any* other building anywhere: it is unique. That would have been a back-handed compliment to Wood, because uniqueness was not admired then as it is today, and because the fact that it remained unique is a demonstration that subsequent architects were not sufficiently impressed by it to pay it the sincerest form of flattery.

In 1771, when taste was changing, Tobias Smollett, in *Humphry Clinker*, made Mathew Bramble (a sort of wishful self-portrait, and therefore probably saying what Smollett himself thought) say that 'The Circus is a pretty bauble, contrived for shew, and looks like Vespasian's amphitheatre turned outside in. If we consider it in point of magnificence, the great number of small doors..., the inconsiderable height of the different orders, the affected ornaments of the architrave, which are both childish and misplaced,...destroy a good part of its effect upon the eye.' In fact the ornaments – the metopes – are neither affected, childish nor misplaced, and the bit about Vespasian's amphitheatre, which has been repeated ever since, was only partially true since the Colosseum is an arched structure, and therefore entirely different from the Circus façade. The only similarities in fact are the use of separate orders on each level and the nearly similar shapes (circular and elliptical). In 1809 Sir John Soane also disliked the Circus, which is not surprising since the inevitable reaction in the see-saw of taste was by then complete. In order to demonstrate its alleged bauble-like character he had a now famous drawing in the Soane Museum prepared for use in one of his lectures to his Royal Academy students. It shows the Circus dwarfed and tiny inside the Colosseum. He said 'it may please us by its prettiness and a sort of novelty, as a rattle pleases a child' but 'the area is so small and the height of each of the orders is so diminutive that the general appearance of the entire building is mean, gloomy and confined.' The criticisms seem to have had no effect whatever on the celebrity of this extraordinary building, which from the moment of its completion has always been one of the most famous spaces in Britain.

Throughout the whole of the twentieth century and much of the previous one, the Circus has been dominated by what, as long ago as 1904, were already being described by Mowbray Green as 'the five immense plane trees' which were planted in about 1820. The enclosed circular space seems to suit the trees, which became immense in a mere 80 years and are truly magnificent specimens now, but the trees don't suit the space. Nobody could deny that seeing them is a most memorable experience, but they disastrously reduce the apparent scale of the architecture, and they obscure much of it. Planes, even as magnificent as these, are quite common, but Wood's architecture is unique. People come from all over the world to see it, not the trees. Arguments as to the desirability of felling them have raged intermittently for years, but the matter is academic in the present climate of arboreal correctness because no city council would dare to face the popular outcry that would result from felling them, or even from debating whether to do so. The London Plane rarely blows down (which is partly why it is used so frequently in towns), and is believed to have a lifespan in excess of three hundred years, so, contrary to what is sometimes said about the rapidly approaching end of these Bath giants, it is likely to be a much later generation which will eventually have to decide how to treat the Circus when they have gone.

John Wood paved the space with setts, apart from a circular cistern in the middle which supplied water to the houses. It was open at first, but soon covered over, and the pavement around the perimeter was stone paved and protected from vehicles by a raised kerb and a row of oak bollards. Originally there was no planting whatever, though by 1820 a shrubbery containing the sapling planes had replaced the cistern. Needless to say, the paved space without the trees and grass looked bigger and better – more like an Italian piazza.

Most writers on The Circus have appreciated the enormous superiority of Wood's version, with its three entrances, over nearly all the subsequent imitations, which have four. In Wood's version your view as you approach is of the houses on the opposite side of the Circus: in its numberless descendants you look down the road going out on the other side. The superiority applies equally when one is standing inside The Circus, where building makes up a higher proportion of the periphery than in the subsequent versions, where the additional road means that there is a higher ratio of gap to building. In Oxford Circus for example, one is much more conscious of the four roads going out than one is of the only partially enclosing buildings. A circus with three exits provides a satisfactory sense of enclosure, one of the same diameter with four does not. What it boils down to is this: a circus with three exits is a circular building – urban planning by an architect – and a circus with four is a road junction – urban planning by a technician.[12]

---

12 For once the English version is much better than the French one. The Place des Victoires originally had six roads running into it symmetrically, and was made worse in 1833 when another was cut into it. Photographs and engravings always flatter it because they invariably focus on the largest of the enclosing segments, thus giving a totally misleading impression.

37 The partial view of the Circus visible from near the top of Gay Street

Gay Street is built on a fairly steep slope that flattens out as it enters The Circus. This means that people coming up Gay Street are unable to see the houses facing them on the far side of The Circus until they are near the top of the slope. (37) Many writers have criticised Wood for this. Quite apart from the fact that any alternative would have been virtually impossible on this topography, the sudden surprise as the houses appear to rise out of the ground as one nears The Circus is a marvellous visual experience.[13] The deliberate achievement of surprise was one of the chief aims of English landscape designers in the eighteenth century. Stephen Switzer, for example, had written in 1718 that the landscape designer 'will endeavour to diversify his views, always striving that they may be so intermixed, as not to be all discovered at once; but that there should be as much as possible, something appearing new and diverting'. Wood's passion for the Druids, and his urge to replace Classical authorities by biblical ones says unmistakably enough that he was a romantic. He was famous for his stern and classical Roman buildings, but their nonconformism and ambiguities are deeply un-classical. The layout of his sequence from the Square to the Circus, and then on to the Crescent, is romantic and picturesque. He was doing for the city what the landscape designers were doing for noblemen's parks.

13 The situation is reminiscent of the great row in 1916 between Edwin Lutyens and Herbert Baker over the approach road to the Viceroy's House at New Delhi. Lutyens wanted a continuous incline so that his building could be seen throughout the enormous length of King's Way. But there was an increase in gradient where Baker was building the Secretariat buildings, which cut off the view of all but the dome. Lutyens wanted this to be cut away. The lesser architect won the argument and Lutyens said he had met his Bakerloo. He never forgave Baker. Arguments as to who was right have continued ever since. I have been to Delhi and looked at the view as one drives up King's Way. I side with Baker.

He died at the age of 49 on 23rd May 1754 'of a long and tedious illness', having laid the foundation stone of the Circus only three months before. So although, as far as we know, it was faithfully completed to his designs by his son, he never saw it himself. Construction of the Royal Crescent, the last of the great sequence of spaces he had begun, wasn't started until 1767, thirteen years after his death. So almost all historians have assumed that it was designed by his son. Unlike the Circus, the Crescent has usually had a good reception from the critics, and has probably always been the most popular building in Bath. It is hard to imagine anybody not responding to those golden arms opened wide to welcome the sun and the visitors. (38) But after that glorious welcome the thing which has always struck everybody who looked at all closely is the contrast in character between the Circus, which is crowded with incident, and the Crescent, which seems sparse. They look like the work of different men. But this immediately obvious difference is not as conclusive a pointer to the son's authorship as people have assumed, since although the north side of Queen Square and several other undoubted works of the elder Wood are also crowded, he designed Prior Park which has a sparseness of detail which is very reminiscent of the Crescent.

If there are superficial differences between the Circus and the Crescent, there are underlying similarities that are typical of the elder Wood. One is that both the Circus and the Crescent display the extraordinary dichotomy between the architect's willingness to lavish expense on those features that give each of them their particular architectural character, and his ingenuity in making savings wherever they will have no damaging visual effects. Another similarity is mentioned by Mowl and Earnshaw: Wood's belief that a temple to the moon goddess had stood on the hill would have given him a powerful incentive to recreate, in stone, her crescent diadem.

Furthermore, in his 1741 book *The Origin of Building or the Plagiarism of the Heathens Detected*, Wood notes that Vitruvius recommended the Ionic order – used on the Crescent – as being appropriate to the moon goddess. Finally, and most convincingly of all, the idea of building a terrace of houses in a crescent was entirely new. From what we know of the two men it seems much more likely that the elder Wood had the necessary inventiveness and the younger one did not. It seems reasonable to suppose that the father had the original idea, drew it out in some detail and chose the order. The younger man, probably about a decade later, then drafted the working drawings and designed all the details.

Once again it is necessary to pause in order to point out that a building (as opposed to a row of houses) in a crescent shape was not new. The shape was inherent in much ancient Roman architecture, and appears at the well-known topmost level at Palestrina; in a fascinating and little known temple at Lambaesis in north Africa; and in so many surviving Roman frescoes that there must, surely, have been many more built examples than we know about. Henri IV's semi-circular Place de France was designed in 1610 to accommodate seven fully detached public buildings, though it was never finished. A crescent was proposed unsuccessfully by Fischer von Erlach in 1704 for a palace for the King of Prussia, and by an anonymous draughtsman in 1720 in an unrealised project for rebuilding Magdalen College in Oxford. There are no doubt other examples, but none that I know for a crescent-shaped terrace of houses.

Because there are now dozens of crescents in Britain, and because they are so familiar to us, it is hard to believe that Wood really invented the idea, and that the Royal Crescent in Bath was the first. His belief that there was once a temple to the Moon Goddess on Lansdown Hill may have acted as a spur to his imagination, but as we shall see, he often had a practical reason to support his theoretical one. He had a very practical reason indeed for the shape of Royal Crescent. Because it is built across a shallow valley, if it had been a straight terrace he would have had to build up the ground in the centre to support it, and not only that but the road serving it as well. In the eighteenth century that was the routine way of dealing with the problem, but Wood realised that if his terrace followed the curve of the contours he could save the high cost of the substructure. He will also have realised that his version is calmer and simpler – more beautiful – than a built-up version could have been. There can be no doubt whatever that this consideration, more than any of the others, was responsible for Wood's invention.

Almost every writer on Bath's architecture has repeated Mowbray Green's statement that the Circus has small-scale details, designed to be seen from close up because the confined space allows no long views, and the Crescent has large-scale details so that they can be appreciated from a distance. The argument is far from convincing. The 96.9m diameter of the Circus is almost exactly the same as the width of Queen Square, and Wood didn't feel the need to use small-scale detail there. Furthermore, people who live in the Crescent, and their visitors, all see it most often from the pavement immediately in front of their houses, and their appreciation of it at that time is at least as important as when they are more rarely looking at it across the great lawn. It is much more probable that the reason for the marked difference in the two façades is that Wood wanted all three of the set pieces in the sequence, Queen Square, Circus and Crescent, to be as different from each other as possible.

The architectural system of the Crescent is very simple. (39) All three storeys are faced with smooth ashlar, which ignores the Palladian pattern of the ground floor being rusticated to give it the apparent strength to carry the giant columns above. All the window and door openings, like those in the Circus, are cut cleanly into the wall without architraves or other enrichments. The ground floor is capped by a large string-course which is in fact the top of a great stylobate (or platform) on which the columns sit. This means that the face of the upper floors is set back about 70cm from the face of the ground floor. The three-quarter columns between each window support a massive entablature, and that in turn supports a balustrade. The height from the pavement to the top of the balustrade is 12.5m. In Italy those dimensions would be unremarkable, but in England they count as very grand architecture.

The Crescent is as unconventional, and in its own way almost as odd, as the Circus. The unending row of closely spaced giant columns (only 1.8m apart at their bottoms) suggests great richness, which is curiously denied by the lack of rustication, or of any small details apart from the balustrade and the Ionic capitals of the columns. There is no other ornament whatever, everything is smooth stone, even the columns are unfluted. The effect from close-up is a strangely cold and impersonal architecture, only made warm by the lovely colour of the stone. The use of the great Roman colonnade and the refusal to give the building any superficial charm of ornament makes the Crescent an impressive example of European Neo-Classicism. Wood started as a good Palladian but finished as one of the first to react against the style and its restrictions.

Another respect in which the Crescent is like the Circus (and unlike Palladian buildings) is that it has no emphasis at its centre or ends. It is simply an enormously long colonnade without pediments or projecting pavilions. At least that is the appearance, but when you look closely (and only when you do) you see that at each end the columns are doubled, and in the middle the central intercolumniation is slightly wider than the others and the columns on either side

39 Royal Crescent. Designed by John Wood the elder, and built with minor but ill-judged variations by his son John in 1767, 13 years after his father's death. Every window has lost its glazing bars

of it are also doubled. (40) These paired columns are not set forward or back, or differentiated in any way from all the others, but take their place in the row, merely throwing out the rhythm so slightly that the incidents are almost imperceptible and therefore wasted. But the doubling of the columns at the centre has a result that would never have been accepted by the elder Wood, because one of each pair has to occur over a ground-floor window. To impose a great point load over an opening in a wall is the ultimate sin against structural logic. Finally, in a despairing attempt to give the central non-event a bit more punch, the younger Wood (for surely he is the culprit) arched the first floor window between his paired columns. It is another minute gesture, utterly lost in that huge façade. As an attempt at central and end emphases these little variations are useless because they don't emphasise anything: you have to search for them. They are pathetic, so incompetent that they must surely be a last-minute afterthought, added by the son just before building began, in a sudden panic that this enormous unrelieved façade designed by his father would be monotonous. In fact it isn't monotonous, partly because of its enormous dignity and grandeur, and partly because something really important does change – the curvature. At its centre the Crescent has a very shallow curve, but towards the ends the curve of the ellipse becomes much more acute, so that the last house at each end has turned 90 degrees to face its counterpart at the other end.

40 Royal Crescent. The younger Wood's introduction of an arched window makes no impact on the Crescent as a whole – as he intended it to do – but it does give an added sparkle to the central house.

The great colonnade turns at each end onto the flank walls of these two end houses, making them into very grand entrance façades. (41) At the corners the columns are doubled, making a cluster of three. The columns don't continue uninterruptedly across the façades as in the rest of the Crescent, but leave a wide gap in the middle, thus avoiding the solecism of a central column bearing down on the entrance doorway. This arrangement, with all the visual weight at the outer corners, means that they pull outwards very strongly. In theory this should be disturbing, ugly, but through some magic it isn't: it is strangely beautiful. So who designed it, father or son? Only great architects can occasionally pull off tricks of this sort: a fair guess is that the father had drawn the elevation of the Crescent showing these end houses as they were

41 Number 1 Royal
Crescent

built. Construction of the Crescent began with No 1 at the eastern end, so it is highly probable that the younger, more rule-bound Wood was unhappy when he saw it completed, and resolved to try something different when construction got to the centre of the Crescent, with the result we have seen.

Nowadays the ineffectual fiddling about at the centre and ends of the Crescent is noticed by few people and has no effect whatever on its beauty, but in the eighteenth century educated

42 Royal Crescent. Drawing room of number 1

people respected the rules of architectural composition as much as today they respect, say, the rights of minorities. Infringement then was as shocking as a racist comment today. *The Stranger's Assistant and Guide to Bath* of 1773 said 'The wretched attempt to make a centre to the Crescent where none was necessary is absurd and preposterous, in a high degree. The pairing of the pillars is too small a difference to be noted in so large a building, as is the window intended to be the centre, and the former of these circumstances has led them into an egregious solecism, viz., that of placing a window under each pair of pillars.' Estimates of the younger Wood's ability as a designer all depend on whether he designed the Crescent or not. If we put the Crescent aside, his other known buildings, as well as the plates in his book of cottage designs, are no more than respectable. It seems likely that if he had not been his father's son – and namesake – we would think of him only as a minor Bath architect.

Although the leases of the Circus and Crescent make plain that builders were free to do what they liked behind Wood's elevations, the way the tapering shape of each house in the Circus is resolved must surely be due to Wood. Instead of the trapezoidal rooms which are the usual and unwelcome result of building terrace houses on a curve, here the divergence from the rectangular is taken up by wedge-shaped party walls. On page 68 is a fascinating plan drawn by Walter Ison for his great *Georgian Buildings of Bath* of 1948. (44) It shows three adjoining houses with totally different plans, all fitted with enormous skill behind their identical façades. Either their builder was very clever or he employed Wood to plan them for him.

Gay Street, which connects Queen Square to the Circus, and Brock Street, (45) which connects the Circus to the Royal Crescent, are the linking passages between the three themes of Wood's composition. In crudely practical terms they accommodate the less expensive but still respectable houses that were essential to balance the really expensive ones. As we have seen, Wood was good at transmuting practical and economic necessities into aesthetic opportunities. In both linking streets he, and later his son, could relax their control slightly. If one owner wanted a more elaborate façade, as happened at 8 Gay Street, (32) they could allow it without causing a significant disturbance of the pattern. When either of the Woods wanted to give access to further streets of houses they could have side roads going off wherever it was most convenient, rather than at specific points which the architecture dictated. This proved to be necessary in both linking streets.

As one goes westwards along Brock Street towards the great lawn there is little indication of what awaits one around the corner. The surprise, as the immense Crescent is suddenly revealed, is even greater than when arriving at the top of Gay Street. Eighteenth-century wits made much fun of the absurdity of planning elaborate 'surprises' in landscape gardens which could only serve this function the first time they were seen. Their ridicule had no appreciable damping effect on the desire of garden owners to have them. In Bath, and in countless gardens, one can see why. No matter how many times one has approached the Circus from Gay Street and the Crescent from Brock Street, fully knowing what awaits one, the final revelation is still an enchantment.

It is constantly fascinating to observe the shrewd way in which Wood saved money wherever he could, whilst lavishing it on splendour that no other English builder had ever considered appropriate for rows of speculative houses. One final instance must be described because it shows how clearly he understood the way people perceive buildings, and then took advantage of it. A curved wall can be built of uncurved bricks because the units are so short that the resultant faceting is imperceptible. Wood, like most architects of his time, liked to use large blocks of ashlar, a fact he mentions in his *Essay*. If they were used with flat faces in a curved

43 Stair in the Royal Crescent Hotel. Cantilevered stairs of this type were very popular throughout the Georgian period. The treads were bedded into the wall and cantilevered out from it. Each tread depends for its support on the one below, which in turn depends on the one below that, and so on down to the bottom. Remove one and all above will collapse

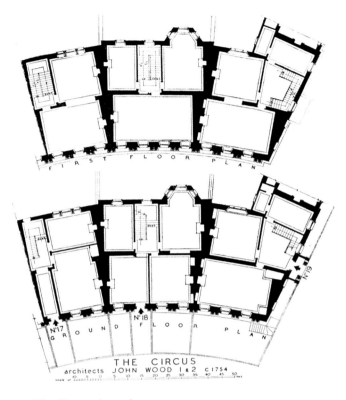

44 The Circus, plans of
numbers 17-18.
From Ison

wall the faceting would be extremely ugly, so each one would have to be cut on the curve. Even in the eighteenth century when labour was cheap, that was very expensive. So in the Circus and the Crescent the Woods built the front walls of each house in flat lengths and masked the resulting angles between them by the columns. The main horizontal lines, however – the three entablatures on the Circus, the huge entablature on the Crescent and the great string-course below its columns – were built of curved stones. If you look carefully, the flat lengths of wall and the flat windows in them are apparent, especially in the Crescent, but very few people look at buildings with such care. Most of us see the things Wood intended us to see – the genuinely curved main horizontal lines – and we unconsciously assume that everything else is also built on the curve. That makes one think again about the columns, so expensively positioned between every window in the Circus and the Crescent. The expense doesn't seem so great when one realises that in addition to giving great richness to the façades, each one (or in the Circus, each pair) is masking an ugly junction in the wall, and thereby making possible a substantial saving in the cost of the stone cutting.

It is perhaps worth pausing to consider further whether the Circus and the Crescent are truly Palladian, as so often claimed. If they are it can only be by extending the concept to include them. Such categories, from Gothic, through Impressionism to Post-Modernism, are all the invention of historians or critics. They are indispensable but basically ridiculous, because buildings and other works of art have to be shoe-horned into one or other of them, regardless of fit. There is nothing in the work of Palladio himself, or of Inigo Jones and his followers, which is like either the Circus or the Crescent. The nearest parallel is not with Palladio, but with Sansovino's Library of St Mark in the Piazzetta at Venice, which is crowded with highly disciplined incident like the Circus, and has no central or end emphases like the Crescent. Although it was greatly admired by Palladio nobody has ever called it Palladian, so it has to be put into the box called Mannerism (as, ridiculously enough, the work of Palladio is often squeezed). The Circus and the Crescent fit into no box, they are unique. Wood's early work is Palladian, his posthumously completed work is not.

It is easy to forget that, as with all architects, Wood's day-to-day concerns were necessarily down to earth: he will have spent much more time worrying about costs than cornices. The wonder is that as far as one can judge he never let it deflect him. It is hard enough to persuade backers to finance the most routine house-building ventures, even when what is proposed has been done successfully time and time again, but Wood was proposing something entirely new.

Queen Square, the Circus and the Crescent could not have been built without the co-operation of a large number of people, primarily small building tradesmen and their mortgagors, but also their customers. All or most of the first group and many of the second lived in Bath, and all were prepared to risk substantial sums of money on Wood's plan. The Bath that they created, which was to influence the city planning of princes, was the work of a substantial proportion of the tradesman and professional class of what was clearly a very remarkable community.

45 Brock Street

Apart from Queen Square the influence of Wood's strictly architectural design was not great. The elevational treatments of his most imitated street forms, the Circus and the Crescent, were too quirky and individual to become general models for imitation. After two and a half centuries it is clear that Wood was an architect of national status, and an urban planner of world class. By 1775 when the Royal Crescent was completed, Beau Nash had been dead for 14 years and the elder Wood for 21. Just as Nash had taught the English middle and upper classes to behave together decorously when assembled in social gatherings, so Wood and his son had taught them to live in houses that behaved together decorously when assembled into streets and towns. Neither Nash nor Wood achieved those transformations on their own, but their contributions were great.

5 Hill climbing

The internal planning of English terrace houses was more or less standard throughout the eighteenth century, though the styles of decorating and furnishing them changed greatly over the years. Every household employed servants who slept in the garrets or occasionally even in the kitchen, which, with its associated rooms, was in the basement. After about 1770 it became common for the rooms to be wired to a row of bells in the basement so that servants could be summoned. The coal cellar was under the pavement and the coal was shot into it through the stone, or later cast-iron, cover set in the paving. Tradesmen made their deliveries to the door in the sunken 'area' at the front of the house, reached by a gate and steps down from the pavement. On the ground floor the family and their visitors entered the front door into a small lobby which, until the wide use of decorative fanlights in the last third of the century, was usually unlit, though a few had undecorated 'over-door' glazing. The lobby's inner door entered into the stair hall. Off this were the dining or eating room (the terms were interchangeable) at the front and a parlour at the back. In the better terrace houses the stairs had turned mahogany bannisters and rails which swirled round at the bottom to form a buttress. In the cheaper houses the bannisters were of pine, the handrails of pine faced with mahogany and the bottom swirl usually omitted, particularly in Bath. Pine, with the exception of floor boards, was always painted, mahogany never was. On the first floor the ceilings were almost invariably higher than those on the floor below. The drawing room usually occupied the whole width of the front, and a sitting room and the stair occupied the back. The rooms were interconnected by a pair of wide folding doors set in an arch in the intervening wall. In the drawing room it was usual to hang mirrors – pier glasses – on the piers between the windows. Floor boards were dry-scrubbed with fine sand or fullers' earth. They were rarely polished and never varnished. From the 1730s and 1740s carpets were increasingly common. They were sold by the yard in strips and then sewn together and finished off with a border. Inlaid floors or borders were rare in terrace houses. The main bedrooms were on the second floor and the children's and servants' rooms in the garrets lit by dormer windows. There were no bathrooms. Water for washing was carried up to the bedrooms by servants, and chamber pots carried down by them for emptying into the privy at the rear. There was nothing embarrassing about this.

As explained in the last chapter, the walls of the reception rooms in most terrace houses were proportioned so that the dado represented the pedestal of a column, and the wall above represented the column and its cap. Above this were plaster versions of an entablature and cornice, or more frequently, of the frieze and cornice alone. Doors were framed by moulded wooden architraves which projected far enough from the wall surface to allow the skirting and dado rail to stop against them neatly. Windows were framed by architraves of the same pattern, forming boxes into which the shutters were folded. In the first half of the eighteenth century the reception rooms were occasionally wainscotted as in previous centuries, but this came to be seen as old-fashioned, and the walls were plastered and covered with silk or wallpaper above the dado rail. Below it the wall was painted, usually a paler colour than the silk or paper above. The painted skirtings, in addition to representing the base of a pedestal, were a protection against scrubbing brushes and brooms, and the dado rails, representing the cornice of a pedestal, were a protection against knocks from the backs of chairs. Most eighteenth- and nineteenth-century town houses were rented rather than owned by their occupiers, however rich, because it made moving house easier. Ownership became more common at the end of the nineteenth century, made possible by the new building societies.

Before the opening up of Bathwick by the building of Pulteney Bridge, all the available building land was to the north of the city, sloping quite steeply up from the Circus and the Crescent, and precipitously down to the river on the east. Inevitably the most fashionable lodgings were on the more expensive but easier ground, and the less fashionable on the cheaper but most difficult, which ran along the London Road, and was possibly blighted to some extent by its traffic. The first terrace to be built on this land was the quite short Bladud's Buildings which was started in 1755 and slowly grew northward until 1762 when it was brought to a close by an ancient right of way which still burrows under the houses and steps precipitously down to Walcot Street. Four years later, in 1768, work on the terrace started again, this length being called The Paragon, though the two are in reality one tediously long building. (46) Because it is built along a gently curving contour it is level from end to end. On its downhill side it hangs dramatically above Walcot Street, with its great retaining wall forming one of Bath's many accidentally achieved bits of picturesque scenery. (47) Although the terrace is much too long, the individual house fronts were pleasantly designed by Thomas Atwood (c.1733-1775), a wealthy plumber who was a city councillor and, to cries of rage from his competitors, a member of its influential Building Committee. He gave each house a little individuality by a pedimented doorway and a pedimented central window on its first floor. If this terrace were in Birmingham or Manchester it would be locally celebrated and occupy a proud place in the guide books, but in Bath it is of minor interest, simply a row of decent Georgian houses gently curving as it follows its contour. It now forms the east side of an unpleasant traffic-dominated canyon (with the horrible characteristic of amplifying noise, such as the sirens of the fire appliances rushing from their depot in Cleveland Place to fires in the city). The miscellaneous houses along the uphill western side of the road have only minor interest, but there is one welcome gap where the Countess of Huntingdon bought the largish site on which to build her 1765 gothick Chapel, set back from the pavement and fronted by the delightful battlemented and ogee-arched little house for the minister. This interlude, now housing the Building of Bath Museum, is a welcome relief from the interminable rows of routine houses facing and flanking it.

Further north along the London Road, also on its western uphill side, is Walcot Parade of

46 The Paragon.
Thomas Atwood,
1755-62

around 1770, a terrace which curves irregularly, and steps down irregularly, and because of the steep cross-slope is set on a pavement raised high above the road. (48) The pavement snakes up and down in a great curve following its own line, different from either the slope of the houses or the slope of the road. As architecture the Parade is routine, as picturesque scenery highly enjoyable, but alas now spoilt by traffic.

It is very hard to imagine central Bath as it was at this time, when the occupants of most of the fashionable houses, those in Wood's developments on Lansdown Hill, could reach the hot baths and Assembly Rooms only through a series of lanes and the yard of an inn. The first step to plug them properly into the city was the building of Milsom Street, and at its top Edgar Buildings built at a right angle to it. Both of them were started in 1761. The houses in Milsom Street, most of which have now lost their ground floors to shops, were designed, probably by Thomas Atwood, on similar lines to Bladud's Buildings, but with slightly more refined details. They had to step up the slope, but Edgar Buildings, being built across it, could be designed as a level terrace with a pedimented centre and projecting pavilions at each end. The central

47 The backs of The Paragon hanging over Walcot Street. Dramatic urban scenery such as this is one of hilly Bath's great visual pleasures

48 Walcot Parade c.1770. Another example of Bath's classical architecture forced by the topography into picturesque scenery

49 The central pavilion of Edgar Buildings designed to close the view up Milsom Street. Probably by Thomas Atwood, 1761

pavilion neatly terminates the view looking up Milsom Street. (49) Twenty years later the uniformity of Milsom Street was broken but hugely improved by the building of Somerset Buildings, five houses designed as a single composition – of which more later.

Each morning the people lodging in the Circus or the Crescent had to walk, or pay to be carried in sedan chairs, for their attendance at the Hot Bath at the bottom of the hill, and on Assembly evenings had to repeat the procedure to attend the Rooms, also down in the town. Clearly this was not helping the prospects of further development up the hill, so in 1765 John Wood the younger, displaying initiative worthy of his father, invited a group of potential investors to meet at his house to discuss building a new and larger set of Rooms on a site north-west of Queen Square. Because of disagreement about whether or not the Rooms should include a tavern, the meeting was abortive, but after a design by Robert Adam on a site just to the east of the Circus had been turned down because of its over-ambition and great cost, Wood tried again, producing a more modest design on the site proposed by Adam, which was accepted. The city having lost the chance of gaining a major building by the greatest living British architect, Wood then tragically missed another opportunity. He had under his control a huge parcel of land onto which he had to plan the largest modern public building in Bath and several speculative terraces of houses. It was a dream opportunity to design them together as an ensemble that could again have put Bath into the forefront of urban design in Britain, perhaps in Europe. Certainly the site was difficult, sloping down to the south. No doubt there were other difficulties we cannot know about, but he failed dismally to rise to the opportunity, or even, perhaps, to recognise that it existed. Apart from the fact that two of the terraces are parallel to the Rooms, there is no relationship between terraces and Rooms whatever, not even some architectural feature smiling across to another opposite. Even the entrance to the Rooms is clumsily positioned, facing onto the chaotic backs of the houses in the Circus. If one examines the plan of the building it is clear that Wood could easily have reversed it without disturbing the layout of its rooms in any significant way. Instead of entering on the west side, the entrance could have been on the east where it would have faced onto the end of one of his terraces. It would not have required much skill or forethought to have designed that end of the terrace so that it responded formally to the Room's entrance. None of this was to be: Wood designed each building pleasantly but the thought of designing them as a coherent group apparently never entered his head: unlike his father, he was no urban planner.

Funding for the Rooms came from a Tontine subscription, whereby 53 investors took shares of the profits each year until their death. When that occurred their share went into the common pot, so that each person's share grew as investors died, one lucky but aged individual finally scooping the lot. (It is said that tontines were eventually made illegal after a series of suspicious deaths.) Wood laid the foundation stone in 1769 and work was completed in 1771.

Externally the building is imposing but somewhat stolid, not spectacular as Adam's would surely have been, and slightly out of date, being still largely Palladian in its details. Unable to afford a grand frontispiece with columns and a pediment, or even any decorative carving, Wood nonetheless produced a large and dignified building depending for its effect on its massing, its windows and its fine ashlar masonry. The best elevation, the south, faces onto his Alfred Street. (50) It has simple sashes at ground level, tall architraved and pedimented sashes enriched by balustrades on the first floor and small square windows on the second floor. The north elevation, (51) facing onto his Bennett Street, is simpler, the first-floor windows have no balustrades and there are no windows at second-floor level. The building is capped all round by a fine modillioned cornice and a balustraded parapet. Built against the north front is a long single-storey colonnade with arched windows, which was a sort of garage for sedan chairs. The building is impressive, magisterial in its simplicity and powerful presence, but disappointing because of its formless setting.

These Assembly Rooms, inevitably called the New or Upper Rooms to distinguish them from the old Assembly Room of 1706, were burnt out by incendiary bombs in 1942, leaving only the walls standing. Fortunately the most precious furnishing, the great cut-glass chandeliers, had previously been removed to safety, but everything else was destroyed. The damage was so severe that after the war it took the City Council and the National Trust (which by then owned it) eleven years of discussions to decide whether to demolish or rebuild it. However, in 1956-63 the building was restored, it is said faithfully, to what it had been in the eighteenth century, though Mowbray Green's 1904 plan, which includes Victorian internal alterations, suggests that in

removing them the restorers may have lost some of Wood's original arrangements.

It appears that all the main rooms are based on proportions recommended by Palladio (see chapter 3), though it is difficult to be certain because it seems possible that in the 1950s rebuilding, the heights of ceilings etc. were unwittingly altered by a few inches here and there. Visitors enter a wide vestibule which projects forward from the building and leads to the splendid top-lit octagonal lobby which gives access to the three great public rooms. The lobby is lit by a lantern on a high octagonal dome resting on Doric columns and pilasters. Entered on the left from the Lobby is the huge and splendid Ballroom. (52) Its height is equal to its width, and its length is two and a half times its width: all proportions recommended by Palladio. A heavy frieze moulded with a Vitruvian scroll runs right round the room at first-floor height, supporting Corinthian half columns. Above is an entablature and over that another frieze. Over the entrance from the lobby is a great apsidal musicians' gallery.

Entered on the right from the lobby is the Tea Room with height equal to its width and length two and a half times its width. (53) This room also has a great moulding running round the room at first-floor level, supporting Corinthian half-columns which become free-standing when they front the huge musicians' gallery which runs across the room at its western end. On the gallery's back wall the columns are responded by Corinthian pilasters. The gallery is supported on shorter, stubbier, Ionic columns with responding pilasters on the wall behind.

Immediately ahead of the lobby is the great Octagon Room, 48 feet in diameter, entered under its musicians' gallery. It has marble fireplaces in alternate sides with rococo looking-glasses over them. Above is a frieze of running acanthus scroll, and high above, the entablature from which the dome's octagonal ceiling rises to the roof.

If these interiors had been designed by Robert Adam the decorative plasterwork would have been picked out in colour and gilding, and the walls painted in rich and varied colours. Contemporary engravings and watercolours show that there was little of such richness in the Assembly Rooms. The Victorians found the simple treatments inadequate and beefed them up with richer colours and stencilled ornament, painting the columns a darker colour than the walls against which they stood, putting statues and vases in the Ballroom's niches and painted versions of them on the other walls. In old photographs it looks magnificent, but it was all destroyed in 1942. In the 1970s the interior decorator David Mlinaric decorated the rebuilt principal rooms, basing his scheme, it is said, on colour samples preserved in the City Archives, though today it seems remarkably 1970s-ish and, compared to the Victorian photographs, disappointingly dull.[1] Nonetheless, the interiors are glorious. When they were crowded with dancers in scintillating costumes and filled with music and laughter, as they were designed to do, they must have been wonderful. The younger Wood could be justifiably proud.

51 Assembly Rooms, north and entrance fronts

1 Even when they try to do otherwise, designers and artists always reflect the taste of their own period. I have little doubt that that is what happened here.

52 Assembly Rooms.
Ballroom

The decision to build the Assembly Rooms guaranteed a surge in demand for nearby lodgings. This gave Wood the encouragement to build, concurrently with the Rooms, the streets mentioned earlier, Alfred Street on their south side, Bennett Street on their north, and Russell Street running uphill from Bennett Street. In Alfred Street, divided into two by Bartlett Street, the steep cross fall meant that the basements on the uphill side could be at ground level on the south-facing garden side. The easternmost of the two terraces had the by then routine treatment of a pedimented centre. On the north side of the Rooms, Bennett Street, (54) stepping irregularly up to Belmont, has little architectural distinction as a terrace, but each of the south-facing house fronts, though like hundreds of others in the new streets, have enough charm to have made them desirable then and ever since. Most of the houses in Russell Street have a feature which became popular in these years, a Venetian window in their first-floor drawing rooms. Other terraces of this period, such as Belmont, also have a few but they are not visible from the street because they are on the garden side to enjoy wide views over the countryside, rather than of the houses on the opposite side of the road. One of Russell Street's most attractive features is the termination at the top, showing that the younger Wood did occasionally see such opportunities. The view looking up is closed by the three-storey canted bay of a house in his Rivers Street, which he obviously designed for the purpose. (55) The view looking down is closed by the Assembly Rooms, though not on any feature in it, which is what his father would surely have arranged.

THE CLASSICAL BUILDINGS OF BATH

53 Assembly Rooms.
Tea room

54 Bennett Street

Now that Bath's Georgian streets are permanently lined with parked cars it is not easy to appreciate their splendid proportion of width to height. In Ison's 1940s photograph of Russell Street there is just one parked car, and the proportions are gloriously clear to see. Palladio gave no suggestions about the proportions of streets, apart from saying in his third book that in hot countries they should be proportionately narrow to keep out the sun, and in temperate climes wide to allow it in. In eighteenth-century Britain more compelling reasons for wanting to have wide streets in the new parts of towns was their contrast to the narrow and crooked streets in the old parts, and an English love of privacy which requires a decent distance between opposite windows.

A second example of the younger Wood's inability to relate one development to another architecturally is Catharine Place which he built in the late 1770s to the north of Brock Street. (56) It is a sort of narrow square, two stepped terraces facing each other across a small central garden, but with no carefully planned termination at the top as at Russell Street. Since the terrace which crosses at the top is in Rivers Street which Wood was building at the same time, one would suppose that he could have designed a couple of its houses to focus on Catharine Place. It is impossible now to know why he didn't do so. Possibly the dates of building didn't coincide nearly enough, possibly he didn't think of it.

Wood didn't control all the land in this area. Between 1768-73 the bottom of Lansdown Road

was developed by an unknown architect, with Oxford Row on its west side, and the more attractive Belmont opposite. (57) Belmont owes its attraction to the fact that it is raised picturesquely above the traffic on vaults which support a wide pavement onto which its front doors open, but also to the fact that its stone façades glow in the afternoon and evening sun. During most of the day Oxford Row seems glum in comparison.

For more than a decade Rivers Street was the northernmost boundary of the built-up area, until in the 1790s the last of Bath's Georgian squares, St James's, was built immediately north of the Royal Crescent. It differs from most of the previous building speculations in that the speculators, a small group of building craftsmen, employed an architect to make their design, instead of the designer himself being the speculator. The architect was the gifted John Palmer (c.1738-1817), who was shortly to become the City Architect[2] and is now best known for his superb Lansdown Crescent. His design for the Square was probably made in 1790, and most of the houses were complete three or four years later. The sloping site was rectangular and so shaped that the long sides had to step upwards (58) and the short sides could be built along the contours without stepping. (59) The layout of the approach roads which enter at each corner was particularly intelligent. Instead of continuing the line of the four internal roads, they are set at an angle of about 120° to them, so that the views in and out are of terraces sloping off at an angle. This is surprisingly pleasant and gives the Square a much greater sense

2 At that time, and for many years to come, the City Architect remained free to work independently as an architect or as a developer. Needless to say, this caused many complaints from developers who were disadvantaged by their competitor's inside knowledge and influence.

of enclosure than the hundreds of others in Britain where each of the approach roads gives views into and then out beyond the square. Palmer had obviously learnt a lesson from Wood's Circus where the three roads do the same thing.

In 1948 Ison wrote of St James's Square: 'there has been wholesale removal of glazing bars from the windows, and the general effect has not been improved by the pernicious practice of painting in bright colour the ground storey of some of the houses.' That has now been corrected, the disfiguring nineteenth and early twentieth century soot has been washed away, the railings of the central garden which were removed during the war, have been replaced, and the Square, free from the traffic which ruins Queen Square, is the best preserved and maintained square in Bath.

By the 1790s Palladianism had long been dead and under the influence of Robert Adam and others, buildings were being designed with a new lightness and elegance. John Palmer was one

58 St James's Square,
John Palmer, 1790-94.
One of the elaborated
houses in the middle
and at each end of the
two sloping sides

of the first to introduce this refinement, rather belatedly, to Bath. His terraces forming the top and bottom of St James's Square, which don't require stepping, are almost identical to each other and organised conventionally with emphasised ends and centres. The ends, instead of being flat-fronted, are curved into bows, a feature pioneered in Bath a few years earlier by Thomas Baldwin in his Somerset Buildings in Milsom Street. On their first floors the bows have Venetian windows framed by Corinthian pilasters sitting on the first-floor cill bands. Each of the centrepieces has a pediment supported by four Corinthian pilasters. The whole composition is tied together by five horizontal bands – the plinth, a string course over the ground-floor windows, a cill band under the first-floor windows, another string course which rides over the arches of the three Venetian windows, and finally the crowning entablature. The result is slightly disappointing because it is too flat: the centre and end pavilions and their pilasters don't project enough. The same criticism can be made of the stepped terraces

at the sides, where the emphasised centre and end houses, although themselves beautiful, are too weak to control the terrace where the real dominating feature is the stepping. Palmer was quick to learn. His next terrace had bolder and more effective features.

St James's Square was built during a nation-wide speculative housing boom lasting from the late 1780s to 1793. During such booms land becomes expensive and finance plentiful. The result is that sites which are distant from shops and other amenities, or on slopes so steep that they are disproportionately expensive to develop, suddenly seem to be reasonable prospects. Difficulties, which in normal times would deter speculators, evaporate in the sunshine of the bankers' smiles. So, while work at St James's Square was proceeding, a land valuer called Charles Spackman, who had made a fortune in Bath as a coachbuilder, determined to make another by building on some very steep land much higher up the hill. Like most speculators in every boom, he did it with borrowed money. In this instance most of it came from one of the partners in the Bath Bank which, although founded only twenty years before, had been the first bank to be established in the city. By 1790, at the height of the mania, there were six

of these novel institutions in the city, all desperately and dangerously competing to lend money to housing speculators.

60 Lansdown Crescent.
John Palmer, 1789

He employed Palmer to design Lansdown Crescent, (60) which was started in 1789 and finished in 1793, a few weeks after the inevitable financial collapse, so Spackman was lucky, though at least one of the builders was ruined. Palmer appears to have been responsible for rather few buildings, most of those he did build being in Bath. Lansdown Crescent was his best by far, and it is on that that his reputation largely depends. Spackman could scarcely have chosen a more difficult site. It had the usual cross fall along its entire length, but an even steeper longitudinal fall at each end. By following the contours Palmer was able to squeeze a level crescent of twenty houses between these ends, but then the land fell away so steeply that any further houses would have to step downwards extremely abruptly. How to make a single composition of all that must have seemed an insoluble architectural problem, but solve it he did. With great ingenuity he designed the Crescent as three physically separated parts. The main part consists of the twenty houses forming the level concave crescent. Then at each end there is a narrow gap giving access to the mews at the rear, followed by a shorter crescent of houses that step down the hill in a convex curve. The whole composition therefore consists of a level central concave with convex curves dropping down at each end. (61)

We must now pause to look again at some of classical architecture's rules because Palmer broke one of them, probably deliberately. As mentioned earlier, they were enforced because untalented designers produce better buildings if they stick to them. One of the most basic was that in a symmetrical composition – and most classical buildings were symmetrical – it looks best if there is something in the centre on which the eye can focus. Nearly 2,500 years ago architects in Greece had discovered that a short colonnade with a central column looked worse than one with a central gap, because the gap, being shadowed and therefore dark, is more telling than the paler columns. So they evolved the rule that short colonnades must have an even number of columns, and looked best if the central gap was slightly wider than the others, making it the obvious place for the doorway. In the seventeenth century architects realised that for a similar reason there should be an odd number of houses in a terrace, so that the central one would be balanced equally on either side. This reasoning even applied to house façades, which, as we noted in examining General Wade's house in chapter 2, undoubtedly look best if they have an odd number of windows on each floor. In Bath's terraces you will occasionally see a house with two or four windows, but the vast majority have three, and a few five. In the eighteenth century every architect and a large number of educated laymen knew the rules, and, as happened at the Royal Crescent, were quick to condemn any architect who broke them. Rules, however, are a challenge, and throughout architectural history the cleverest architects have delighted to find ways of breaking them so brilliantly and convincingly that only the stupid or rigidly academic would complain. (Michelangelo immediately comes to mind. He broke the rules so brilliantly that he changed the course of architectural development, setting it on a new route that led through Mannerism to the Baroque.) For Palmer's generation the most dazzling rule breaker was the supremely gifted Robert Adam. One of his followers, probably Thomas Leverton, had recently built Bedford Square in London with an even number of houses on the north side, marked by a central feature with a pediment supported by five pilasters. He got away with it because the central pilaster provides a perfectly acceptable focus for the eye, but he was much criticised at the time. The pedants did have some justice on their side: after all, why choose to employ an established and formalised system of design if you aren't going to accept its rules?

Stepped terrace houses are more expensive to build than those on the level. Palmer found himself with a central crescent of twenty houses, the absolute maximum he could squeeze onto the level. It is impossible to know whether he knew Bedford Square, but there can be no doubt that he knew that an even number of houses was something he should avoid, because the party wall at the centre would make the necessary central windows impossible. His solution to the problem was different to Leverton's, which had simply ignored the rule, because his drew attention to itself. One is forced to wonder whether he hadn't chosen an even number deliberately to show off his skill.

Architects, when they couldn't or wouldn't avoid the problem, had two standard ways of trying to solve it. The first was to omit a central pavilion altogether. On a short terrace that was fine. On a long one it meant that the terrace had no overall composition and became simply a long row of houses like The Paragon – hardly architecture at all. The second and most nearly

respectable method was to have the correct even number of pilasters, with some blank feature, such as a niche, in the centre where a party wall made a window impossible. That had its difficulties because the niche drew attention to the fact that the architect had got himself into trouble, and it didn't really get him out of it because it was hardly possible to put a niche on every floor, and a single one wasn't strong enough to hold the composition together. He had to find some other feature for the other floors, usually an ornament of some sort. It all tended to look horribly contrived and obvious.

Palmer developed a version of the niche solution. He supported his central pediment correctly on four pilasters, the outer interpilastriations (if I may invent a word) one bay wide and the central one two. (62) That was bold of him, since the need to fill the space between the central pilasters was the problem he had to solve, but in normal circumstances it was perfectly canonical, going back, as we have seen, to ancient Greek and Roman temples, where the wider central intercolumniation emphasised the entrance. The Palladians often used it to allow space for a Venetian window over the doorway, and it was a variant of the Venetian window that Palmer

62 Lansdown Crescent, the central two houses

evolved for use on the first floor, substituting a blind arched recess for the usual arched central light. Because the reveals of the recess are as deep as the reveals of the adjoining windows the arch is only slightly shadowed, and being of pale stone is weaker visually than the dark-looking windows on either side. Palmer compensated for this by arching his elaborately guilloche-carved stringcourse over it, thus drawing attention to it.

The partially blind Venetian window on the first floor was, perhaps, a fairly obvious device. The treatment of the central gap below was much less obvious. The ground floor of the whole Crescent is rusticated, and the pilasters supporting the pediment sit on the unmoulded stringcourse above it. Below this stringcourse Palmer created a miniature single-storey Doric portico, again with the central bay wider than the outer two. These outer bays contain the front doors of the two central houses, and the central bay, under the blank recess of the false Venetian window, contains a semi-circular-headed niche. Into the niche Palmer put a tiny but enchanting flourish of crossed wrought-iron arrows. This miniature three-bay centrepiece fits under the central interpilastriation of the larger one above it in the most natural and apparently inevitable way. It is an entire success. Since at least the late 1940s the miniature two-door portico has been painted white, thereby binding it together. It is difficult to know whether this painting is original or some clever person's later brainwave, but it is probably original because Robert Adam painted some of his London porticos white, and Leverton had done the same in Bedford Square. Whichever, this tiny bit of painted wall is brilliantly effective.

One of the minor miracles at Lansdown Crescent is that none of the windows have been lengthened, as they have in so many of the earlier terraces, so that the great horizontal strips of smooth ashlar between the rows of windows are preserved unbroken. Palmer went to great pains to stress his horizontals, adding one that is seen only occasionally on Bath terraces, the continuous but expensive balustrade on top of the cornice. (Wood used one on the Crescent.) Having designed these great horizontal strips of window, wall and balustrade, Palmer was careful to preserve the integrity of their curved surface. Nothing was allowed to disturb it: the three pavilions, and the pediment over the central one, are curved on plan like everything else, and project a mere few inches, just enough to distinguish them, but not enough to interrupt the continuous curve of the Crescent.

The end pavilions are as clever as the central one. (63) Each consists of a slightly projecting house, five windows wide instead of three like all the others, and with the central three windows set into a large segmental bow which projects well forward from the rest of the façade. Because the intervening roads between the concave Crescent and its convex wings are so narrow that they cause no interruption to the undulating flow, the round tower-like bows are positioned at the point of contraflexure, swinging the concave composition around and into the counter curve.

Both wings are built on land that falls away so steeply that they start at a much lower level than the main Crescent, and then step down a metre or more at each house. They are of the

63 Lansdown Crescent.
John Palmer's bowed end
house and Goodridge's
connecting bridge

same elevational pattern as those in the main part of the Crescent, but with some of the horizontal mouldings omitted because they would be superfluous on a non-horizontal, stepped, terrace. Few crescents anywhere are more intelligently thought out. Nobody previously had thought of solving the problem of building rows of houses on steeply undulating ground in this way. The composition of a concave and two convexes was entirely original, it was symmetrical, and where the details departed from classical orthodoxy, they did it so convincingly that few criticisms were made. Above all, Lansdown Crescent was, and thankfully still is, extremely beautiful. A good case can be made for saying that it's the most beautiful crescent anywhere. Its only rival is John Wood's prototype, which is historically much more important, and its weight and solemnity more impressive. There is nothing solemn about Lansdown Crescent, however; it smiles down at Bath, its outstretched arms holding attendant crescents dancing forward at each hand. Two hundred years after it was built it remains miraculously complete and unaltered, still in its setting of trees, precipitous meadow and grazing sheep.[3] (64)

In 1817 the Bath architect John Pinch the elder built Sion Hill Place, a handsome terrace further up the hill. Paying unmistakable homage to Palmer's Crescent, it utilized a version of

3 The sheep are hired by the residents to crop the grass – and enchant visitors. Critical opinion of the Crescent has been extremely varied. Mowbray Green in 1904 scarcely mentioned it, Ison in 1948 was appreciative, saying 'it worthily upholds the fine architectural tradition established in Bath'. In 1958 Pevsner was scathing: he considered the gaps at the wings 'perverse', and the centrepiece 'decidedly awkward and also inadequate'. In 1975 Charles Robertson thought it 'arguably the most successful of Bath's crescents', and in 2003 Michael Forsyth thought the treatment of the centre and the bows at each end weak.

his bow fronts at each end, but with an astylar central pavilion. The house at the western end has a very curious addition, a windowless extension looking rather like the east end of a chapel. It is in fact a picture gallery added in 1936 by the wealthy Ernest Cook who was mentioned in chapter 4. Around the corner its west-facing end wall is the John Wood façade he had salvaged from Chippenham. (20)

Three years before the completion of Lansdown Crescent in 1793, the architect, builder and rent collector John Eveleigh (dates unknown, probably about 1740-1810) working with a group of speculating builders, began the construction of Somerset Place, a concave crescent which continues in a reverse curve the convex line of Lansdown Crescent's western subsidiary just up the hill from it. Work went slowly and was overtaken by the crash, when it ceased. Many years later, in around 1820 and probably after Eveleigh's death, it resumed briefly but was never finished, leaving a somewhat wider than intended gap between Eveleigh's Crescent and the rise up to Palmer's. The result of the two developments when seen on a map or from the air is a very long serpentine crescent snaking up, down and across the steeply sloping landscape, but this is not apparent when seen on the ground because the two are built at entirely different levels.

Ison thought that Eveleigh did not originally intend to build a crescent, but only what are now its two central houses. (65) They certainly were built first and stood alone for a while, but it would have been very strange to have designed a pair of narrow houses to stand isolated in the

64 Pastoral Bath

65   Somerset Place, the centre two houses. John Eveleigh, 1790

precise centre of a wide and expensive plot. What is more, their huge broken segmental pediment is far too big for a pair of semi-detached houses, and there can be little doubt that they were intended from the first to be the centrepiece of a crescent. Either Eveleigh's site didn't allow him to build his crescent on the level, or, more probably, he didn't want to. A year or two earlier, at nearby Camden Crescent (66), he had hit on an architectural idea for designing a sloping crescent which was a real stinker. There, and now again at Somerset Place, he stepped down the houses one at a time, so that the windows step in groups of three, which is fine. But instead of stepping the cornice and the stringcourse, he built them on the slope, so that they run right through the crescent continuously, sloping down on either side from the centre. That is quite extraordinarily nasty, producing an ugly conflict between the horizontals of the window heads and cills, and the sloping main lines. (67) (It is only fair to record that not everybody finds Somerset Place ugly, and many writers, including Ison, have admired it.) Ison also considered the two pedimented houses in Somerset Place to be 'a design of great beauty and originality'. Original they certainly are, but their beauty is distinctly questionable. The

Adamesque ornaments are pleasant enough if considered on their own, but they are fitted into their architectural setting with little feeling for the shapes they are supposed to decorate. It seems more reasonable to consider the design to be clumsy, naive and ignorant, and a textbook example of duality because the sides of the Crescent look as though they are pulling outwards so strongly they could tear the two houses apart. Eveleigh tried to hold things together by putting a central niche between the first-floor windows and a comic pediment above them, resting its elbows on their cornices. It is much too small to have any binding effect, and the festoon between the second-floor windows is ludicrously ineffectual. The huge gap of the broken pediment, right in the middle of the crescent, is crass in the extreme, seeming to say 'tear here'.

66 Camden Crescent. John Eveleigh, 1788

67 Camden Crescent. The conflict between horizontal and sloping lines

Another awkwardness is the contrast between the flat face of the central two houses, and the curved face of the rest of the crescent, which is not noticeable when seen from a distance, but very jarring when seen in a three-quarter view from the road in front. Even Eveleigh could hardly have done that on purpose, and it was probably due to a change of plan.

In 1941 Lansdown Crescent and Somerset Place were described, and illustrated by a famous aerial photograph, in Siegfried Giedion's *Space, Time and Architecture* as an example of a tradition of undulating forms which included the façade of Borromini's church of San Carlo alle Quattro Fontane in Rome. Giedion's book was extremely influential throughout Europe and the English-speaking world and frequently reprinted, and although he didn't say, or even suggest, that Lansdown Crescent is baroque, his book is the explanation of the constantly repeated and otherwise puzzling description of Lansdown Crescent (and other double-curved buildings in Bath such as the façade of the Cross Bath) as Borrominesque. They are not, and it is highly unlikely that either Palmer or Eveleigh had ever heard of Borromini. If they had they would have disapproved of him very emphatically, as at that time almost every Briton who went to Italy did.

Eveleigh was a very odd man. It seems that he wanted to break every one of classical architecture's rules, and as we shall see, in his only commission for a large country house he even tried – unsuccessfully – to re-invent some of the accepted conventions of house planning. It would be fascinating to know what made him need to do this, but not enough is known about his life to make useful speculations. His most prominent work, Grosvenor Place on the London Road, is a long terrace of 41 houses and a central hotel, which is all that was built of a much more ambitious scheme. Building started in 1791 and ran into the financial collapse which bankrupted him and almost everybody else in the house-building business. Some of the houses were not sold until the 1820s, and isolated bits of decoration were never completed. It is the hotel which catches the eye, as it was intended to do. (68) The basis of the design is conventional: a ground floor rusticated to give it the appearance of solidity and strength needed to support the great weight of the giant Ionic columns and pedestals which stand on it. But there are only seven columns instead of the canonical even number, with the inevitable result that the crushing visual weight of the central column is not supported by the rusticated walling, being positioned instead over the opening which is the hotel's entrance. As noted earlier in the description of the Royal Crescent, a point load positioned over an opening in a wall is the ultimate denial of structural common sense.

The columns themselves are weird. One of the beauties of most columns, whether classical or gothic, is that they lead the eye smoothly up to their caps. There have been occasional exceptions to this, where the column's smooth rise was interrupted by an applied decoration of some sort, but they have been extremely rare and, in the classical examples, always ugly. The Grosvenor Place columns are interrupted three times – once near their bases by wide stone bands, and twice above by ornaments which look as though stuck onto their faces. The bands were probably intended to be carved with similar ornaments, but with Eveleigh one cannot be sure. All three interruptions are extremely jarring. Even the usually plain wall surface between the first- and second-floor windows is interrupted, cluttered by a row of oval medallions (three of which have not been carved). Careful examination of the stone jointing reveals that the large porch is almost certainly a later addition and therefore not by Eveleigh. It certainly doesn't help.

There is nothing calm or classical about this façade. Eveleigh's use of an odd number of columns must have been deliberate rule flouting, but his cluttered columns, though unusual, didn't break any rules: they can only have been the result of an inability to distinguish between the ugly and the beautiful. One is forced to conclude that he broke rules because he was incapable of seeing any aesthetic difference between the result of adhering to them or of breaking them. He had no aesthetic sense. Architecturally, he was a lout, and the perfect example of the value of rules in architectural design. Pevsner called the Grosvenor Place façade 'somewhat vulgar'. He flattered it.

Eveleigh received a few commissions to design and build for other people. He was probably responsible for three terraces in Bristol's Clifton, and was certainly the designer and builder of the large Bailbrook House on the western boundary of Bath. It was begun in 1791, not long before the financial crash which bankrupted him (and also a builder who then took over the contract). The house was finally completed to Eveleigh's design by a third builder in 1800 or 1801. (69) At that time it was usual to build the service parts of country houses as a lower wing to one side or at the back,

68 Grosvenor Place, John Eveleigh. Started 1791 and never finished

often screened from view by planting. Eveleigh managed to persuade Denham Skeet, his lawyer client, to let him build the house as two nearly identical but entirely separate blocks, one behind the other, joined only by an open porte-cochère. The family rooms were in the southern block facing the view, and the domestic offices, servants' accommodation, stables and service yard etc. were in the northern block. This unprecedented and almost diagrammatic separation of functions presumably seemed logical at the time, but it proved to be disastrous. Firstly it meant that the service and servants' rooms had ceiling heights and window sizes much greater than their humble function required, which added enormously to the cost. Secondly, the journey from the kitchen to the dining room, through long corridors and then outdoors through the porte-cochère, meant either that food was cold when it arrived at the table, or it had to be re-heated (and dried-out) in heating ovens outside the dining room. The third fault was less obvious. Both blocks are built on cellars, which, because the house is built on a steep slope, are below ground level in the rear block and at ground level in the family block. This had the advantage of allowing the drawing and dining rooms, which were thus effectively on the first

69 Bailbrook House, John Eveleigh, 1791. The linking entrance hall replaced the earlier porte cochère

floor, to enjoy the magnificent views over the Avon and its water meadows, but the disadvantage that if the family or their visitors wanted to step outside they had to climb down a double flight of steps. By 1800 that was deeply unfashionable. As explained in chapter 1, at that time people everywhere were moving down to the ground floor from their ancestral rooms up on the *piano nobile* in order to obtain the closest possible relationship with nature and their park by being able to step through French doors.

Skeet, for whom the house was built, was forced by the financial situation to sell it before it was completed. Subsequent owners tried to overcome the defects in the design but were never successful. One owner, probably in 1816, removed the steps down from the drawing and dining rooms and built the existing terrace outside the windows, but it was still raised high above the ground. In the mid-nineteenth century the two blocks were united when the porte-cochère was converted into the present entrance hall, but these were palliatives, the house never worked satisfactorily as a family home. The first family to occupy it gave up after only three years and a second family lasted for seven. For the remaining 200 or so years of its existence it has been an institution of some sort, including a home for ten gentlewomen in reduced circumstances, but even that lasted for only seven years. Its most suitable and enduring use, which lasted for 140 years, was as a lunatic asylum. Eveleigh had given his creation the kiss of death.[4]

4 Researching the history of the house was a sobering few days for me. During the long years when it was a lunatic asylum it was run by its owners for profit. The care of some patients in decently sized and sunny rooms was paid for by their families, but pauper patients were paid for by their penny-pinching parish councils. During the worst years, the 1830s and 40s, the Asylum housed nineteen paupers in brutally tiny cells 6'.1" x 5' (1.854m x 1.524m), scarcely larger than a very short bed. The census of 1841 reveals that 103 people, patients and staff, were then resident in the building. That was dangerous over crowding. In 1839

If its hills are a big part of what made Bath famous, as we have seen they are also the greatest difficulty its architects had to face when designing streets on them. The numerous methods they invented for stepping their terraces up and down without infringing the tenets of classicism, or at least without infringing them too far, is a fascinating study. It is a matter of historical significance because what was built in Bath was on exhibition to the nation. Until the closing years of the century almost everybody in society went, at least occasionally, to the spa, and when they got there the main daytime activities were strolling, shopping, visiting and going to see the new buildings. In the eighteenth century Bath was the national academy of street architecture.

The standard way of dealing with a terrace of houses which had to step up a hill was used by the older John Wood in Gay Street, the road which continues the line of the east side of Queen Square. He gave each house its separate length of cornice and stringcourse which simply stop at the party walls. Those of the next house then begin at a higher level. Both Wood and his son used this arrangement in other streets in Bath. Throughout the country it remained for many years one of the standard ways of dealing with the problem, being varied where necessary by having the vertical steps at every second or third house, depending on the slope.

But later, in the decades on either side of 1800, in Bath the most popular way of ordering stepped houses was to sweep each cornice up in a curve to the one above. (70) This was a return to a practice found in big country houses in the less rule-bound baroque years, when up-curved cornices were occasionally used as a means of emphasising the central bays. Its use on a terrace of houses had an entirely different purpose: it was a visual strategem to hold together what the slope of the ground was tending to break apart. It would be interesting to know when it was first used for this purpose. The earliest example I have found is the north side of Castle Street in Bridgwater, though it is likely that there are, or were, earlier ones. Castle Street is a modest brick terrace built as an investment for the Duke of Chandos in 1723-5 by a local builder. No attempt was made to space the windows equally, but instead they are frankly grouped together around the front doors, house by house. Nor is there any attempt to tie the whole terrace together by means of central or end emphases. Cornice, parapet and coping sweep up at each rise in level, which occurs at every second house. The word 'sweep' is almost too dynamic to describe these modest features: they gently curve. Nobody looking at them would suppose that eight decades later they would be taken up again in terrace design, and made expressive. During the rule of Palladianism the upswept cornice and string course were too unclassical – took too great a liberty with one of classical architecture's most canonical parts – for architects to

five patients died within the space of eighteen days. In 1844 an Inspector reported to the magistrates at Wells that the segregation of dangerous, dirty and incontinent patients was unsatisfactory. Nothing was done, it was more important to keep parish rates as low as possible. Things improved slightly in the 1850s, but not much. It is well to remind ourselves that it was not always sunshine behind Bath's golden façades.

70 An example of a terrace in which the cornices and other horizontal lines curve up from house to house. Cavendish Place

want to use them, if indeed they knew of them. It was a work of the Adam brothers which made them respectable. In 1768 the brothers made a design (which was possibly never built) for a three-arched bridge to be built over the river in the grounds of Syon House in Middlesex. It had an entablature and balustraded parapet running horizontally over the arches. As the central arch was wider than those on either side of it, and therefore rose higher, the entablature and balustrade curved up to it and down on the other side. The Adams published the design in the 1773 first volume of their *Works in Architecture of Robert and James Adam*, thus making it widely available. It appears that nobody took up the idea until the 1790s, but when it was revived it was much more commonly used in hilly Bath than in other places. The blundering Eveleigh used it in his huge, ugly and uncompleted 1790s development at Grosvenor, and at the same time Thomas Baldwin used it in Bathwick Street, one of his least successful designs. It is a three-storey terrace with three-light windows on each floor. (71) All the wide windows have entablatures, which somehow make the rows of them look clumsy, an ungainliness which is made much worse by the irregular stepping of the houses. The result is that they look several decades later than the elegant 1790s. In the new century the elder John Pinch (1770-1827) used it much more convincingly on several terraces, almost making a trademark of it.

One of the first was Sydney Place in Bathwick, a four-storey terrace of 1804-8 that forms one of the sides of the unbuilt hexagon of streets he proposed to build around Sydney Gardens. (72) The first thing anybody notices about the building when they see it is the elegance of the details. The ground floor is treated as an arcade supported on piers, each of which has its base and capital. The windows and doors occupy the arches between the piers, the joinery being set inside a broad white-painted stone frame slightly recessed in the masonry arch. The beautiful doorways with narrow lights on either side are progeny of Adam's in London's Mansfield Street.[5] But the leading feature of the design is Pinch's system of curving the cornice and all the other horizontal mouldings upwards from house to house. There are eight of these mouldings, all exquisitely designed, and cut with the most beautiful precision. And all of them curve upward between every house. Because some are close to eye level even the most unobservant person must see and surely enjoy them, as well as the lovely entrance doors and ground-floor windows. (73) The façades of the three pedimented houses are enchanting, with the central window on their first floors set in aedicules of the utmost refinement. The best of Pinch's detailing equals and often surpasses that of any other Bath architect, but his overall compositions were less good. His use of pedimented central and end pavilions was a mistake. There is something utterly ludicrous in the idea of using them 'to group ordinary town houses in such a way as to gain the effect of a single palace', when by stepping up the hill one by one they proclaim so self-evidently that they are a row of separate houses and not a palace. They were a grave error of taste. Possibly it wasn't his, it is quite likely that his client insisted on them to give the houses a higher social standing and thus make them more easily saleable. Yet curiously, they spoil the terrace much more in theory than they do in fact, simply because they are not very apparent. What most people see most of the time – of any building – is the bottom two floors, unless they can see it from a distance, which here they can't, or unless there are powerful vertical elements such as columns, to direct their eyes upward. At Sydney Place there is nothing to take the eyes away

71 Bathwick Street.
Thomas Baldwin,
c.1790

---

5 It is extremely odd that nobody before Adam had thought of doing it. Georgian entrance lobbies in terrace houses, lit only by the fanlight over the door, are always dark. Putting a narrow window on either side of the door whenever the lobby was wide enough, was a great improvement.

72 Sydney Place.
John Pinch the elder,
1804-8. The ironwork
is original

from the delightful lower floors.

In 1808, shortly after he started Sydney Place, Pinch began Cavendish Place on Lansdown, which slopes even more steeply. (74) The front doors and ground-floor windows are different from those in the earlier building, but Cavendish Place also has four storeys, and horizontal mouldings that also curve up at the change of level at each party wall. But there has been no attempt to compose the whole façade by giving it end and central pavilions, and it is all the better for it. The first chapter mentioned the ravages of time upon buildings. Cavendish Place is a rare example of a façade which was almost ruined in the nineteenth century but brought back to its original glory in the twentieth. The most devastating change was the Victorian addition of canopies to the balconies. Most balconies were given them, some were not, some of them were tented, some were flat. They entirely destroyed the terrace's unity. Less damaging, because less miscellaneous, was the addition of sliding louvred shutters to all the windows. At some time in the post-war period all the canopies and shutters were removed. The aesthetic gain was enormous. Raby Place of 1818-25 is another stepped terrace. Of no great distinction, it consists

EXACOMPTA
PARIS

MIXTE
Papier | Pour une gestion forestière responsable
Paper | Supporting responsible forestry
FSC® C002321
www.fsc.org

CUSTOMER RECEIPT

West Hampstead

234 West End Lane West Hampstead London , NW6 1UR

04/01/2025 16:01:10

RECEIPT NO.: 55399

MID: XXX32022   TID: XXXX7140

AID: A0000000041010

Debit Mastercard

XXXXXXXXXXXXX0118

PAN SEQ NO. : 02

SALE :   GBP14.00
TOTAL :   GBP14.00

PLEASE DEBIT MY ACCOUNT

NO CARDHOLDER VERIFICATION

CONTACTLESS

PLEASE KEEP THIS RECEIPT FOR YOUR RECORDS

AUTH CODE:576690

73 Detail of number 94
Sydney Place

74 Cavendish Place.
John Pinch the elder,
1808-1815

of smaller, two-window-wide houses, now also cluttered by balconies on some but not all of them. (75).

Pinch also designed several terraces on the level. The first was Cavendish Crescent, which was started in 1815 but not completed until some years later. (76) Here he had no need to use his trademark upswept mouldings, and most extraordinarily, did not use the pedimented central and end pavilions which he put so pointlessly on some of his stepped terraces, whilst here the design calls out for them. The result is that the Crescent appears to have no endings, and consequently looks unfinished, intended to be continued at each end. Perhaps it was. Pinch didn't make this mistake at Sion Hill Place of 1818-20, which has a pedimented centre and deeply bowed ends. (77)

Possibly Pinch's most delightful terrace is the most humble: St Mary's Buildings off the Wells Road, now on the far side of the railway tracks and always rather removed from the fashionable

75 Raby Place. John
    Pinch, 1818-25

76 Cavendish Crescent.
    John Pinch the elder,
    1815-c.1830.
    The 1996 Cavendish
    Lodge (q.v.) appears on
    the right

77 Sion Hill Place. John Pinch the elder, 1818-20

parts of town. (78) The houses have three storeys and no attics, so they are much smaller than all the others we have been discussing, and they are built on a very steep site that was not at all suitable for retired colonial administrators. They would have been occupied by lower-middle-class people, perhaps modestly successful tradesmen. Apart from some widely spaced and surely superfluous triglyphs, they have no ornament at all, but rely entirely on the proportion of plain wall to the openings in it; to the delightful segmental arches over the ground-floor windows; and to one other feature which, because there are so few others, becomes the most noticeable on this plain façade – the great sweeps of the cornice and its frieze. What had begun, around 1720, as a makeshift contrivance to solve one of the tricky problems that arise when a terrace is built on a slope, has here, around 1820, become the architectural feature that makes this little terrace great.

78 St Mary's Buildings.
John Pinch the elder,
c.1820

6 Bathwick

The 1760s and 1770s saw a revolution in English architecture that had profound effects in Bath. Architects began to accept other authorities than Inigo Jones and Lord Burlington. They looked with new interest at the buildings of the middle ages. The architecture of ancient Greece, previously known only from what Vitruvius had to say about it, could at last be studied at first hand and when engravings of it were published it was a revelation and had an immediate influence. The architecture of more exotic cultures, such as that of China, and later of ancient Egypt and India, were ransacked for new and more exciting motifs. Even the remains of Roman buildings were studied with new eyes, and new beauties discovered. Above all, the buildings of the previous forty years, and their decoration and furnishing, suddenly began to seem intolerably dull and old-fashioned. In Bath, as in Britain as a whole, the work of two architects became the strongest influence on the work of their contemporaries, William Chambers (1723-96) and, above all, his five-years-older contemporary, Robert Adam (1728-92), who has been mentioned here several times already.

Adam, the oldest and most gifted of the four sons of the leading architect in Scotland, had attended Edinburgh University but left before taking his degree to assist his father. When his father died four years later in 1748, he and his brother James took over the practice and associated businesses, and made them so successful that within six years they had made a considerable fortune. This enabled Robert in 1754 to leave for a long visit to Italy, where he worked assiduously to prepare himself for practice in England. His money enabled him to employ the French architect Charles-Louis Clérisseau as a sort of tutor and draughtsman. In 1757 he, Clérisseau and two further draughtsmen crossed the Adriatic to measure and draw the Emperor Diocletian's great palace at Spalato (now Split). After his return to England, in 1764 he published a volume of elegant engravings of their drawings of the palace.

He and his brother James were immediately successful, so much so that in 1773 they were able to publish the first volume of the *Works in Architecture of Robert and James Adam*, followed in 1779 by a second volume, and in 1822 by a posthumous third. The influence of the first two was enormous. Robert, whilst accepting the basic tenets of classical architecture, was prepared to break the Palladian rules when he thought the aesthetic advantage justified it. His buildings were supremely elegant and had what he admired in the work of Vanbrugh – movement – by which he meant the elaborate play of projections forward and back. He had an unerring instinct for the design and placing of ornament based on what he had studied in Roman buildings and surviving frescoes, and in his interiors he displayed an enviable gift for colour. Because of his speed and fluency he was prepared to turn his hand to the design of anything – furniture, silverware, carpets etc. In addition, he and two brothers continued the family building and other businesses. His contemporaries fell upon his building design with enthusiasm, so much so that the next few decades later became known as The Age of Adam.

In fact he didn't have it all his own way. William Chambers was equally successful and an almost equally powerful influence. He was born in Gothenburg where his father, a successful Scottish merchant, was in business. Chambers was sent back to England for his schooling, but when he was sixteen he returned to Sweden and began what his father intended to be a mercantile career. He joined the Swedish East India Company which sent him as a junior officer on voyages to India and Canton. During these years the young Chambers was drawn increasingly to architecture, spending his time in Canton, for example, in drawing temples and pagodas. By the age of 26 he abandoned his nascent mercantile career and began the serious study of architecture. He spent some time in Blondel's École des Arts in Paris and then spent five years in Italy, most of it in Rome, where, like Adam earlier, he received tuition from Clérisseau amongst others. According to Adam, he built a formidable reputation amongst the aristocratic English visitors as a 'prodigy for Genius, for Sense and good taste.' He returned to England in 1755 and commenced practice, soon attracting Royal favour. In 1757 he published *Designs of Chinese Buildings, Furniture, Dresses etc* and the Dowager Princess of Wales appointed him Architectural Tutor to the Prince of Wales, the future George III, and commissioned him to lay out the grounds of her house at Kew and embellish them with the various garden buildings, including the famous Pagoda, which so enrich the Botanical Gardens today. He was on his way. He became enormously successful, was knighted (by the Swedish king but allowed by his old pupil George III to use the title in Britain) and was one of the founders of the Royal Academy which, with Joshua Reynolds, he dominated, but with which Adam had nothing to do. His powerful personality was at the opposite pole to Adam's. His mind and his architectural philosophy were academic. Unlike Adam, he stuck rigidly to architecture, building on tradition and showing how it could be developed. In effect he was the founder of the modern architectural profession. The two men were obvious rivals and were never friends, but in 1791, towards the end of their lives, they worked together in the founding of the Architects' Club. The curious thing is that in some ways their work was similar, but Adam's was always more decorative and elegant, and Chamber's more withdrawn, more austere. In 1759 Chambers published the first part of his *Treatise on Civil Architecture*, followed by further parts in 1768 and 1791. It became the standard architectural manual and remained highly influential into the second half of the nineteenth century, by which time the work of Adam had become unfashionable and widely derided.

By the 1770s Bath had reached a position curiously similar to Edinburgh's at exactly the same time. There, the highly congested city was cut off from nearby fields by the North Loch. In Bath the city was cut off from nearby fields by the river Avon. In both cities the fields were urgently needed for housing, but could be reached only by impossibly long detours. In Edinburgh the problem was solved in 1772 by the opening of the North Bridge; in Bath, by the opening of Pulteney Bridge in 1774. The similarities between the two were remarkable, but there was a profound difference. In Edinburgh it was the town council which had the bridge built, which had previously bought the soon-to-be available land, which held the competition to find a plan for the New Town, and then commissioned James Craig, the winner, to work it up. In Bath all that was done by private enterprise.

That difference had profound effects upon how the two cities look today. In Bath building could only go ahead if each developer felt certain that he would make a profit. Lavish expenditure in making the houses as desirable as he could manage was essential, but could not be justified for anything further. In Edinburgh the Council was often prepared to beautify the new streets and terminate the views up them with great columns, statues on high plinths and other monuments. It is incomparably superior to Bath in that respect. But Bath has two great compensating qualities, the colour of its stone, and more sunshine to make it glow in its radiance.

In 1770, a year after the Royal Crescent was started and six years before it was completed, Pulteney Bridge introduced Bath to a building by Robert Adam. It was that rarest of street types, a bridge lined with houses or shops. Among the small number of other examples now in existence are the Ponte Vecchio in Florence and the Rialto in Venice, but the type was not always quite so rare. In the middle ages this way of producing an income to help repay the heavy cost of building a bridge had been employed wherever the value of land and the demand for houses were high enough to make the additional investment worthwhile – in other words when a bridge was built in the centre of a prosperous city. Old London and Bristol Bridges and the original bridges over the Seine at the Ile de la Cité are examples. In all those cases the widths of the carriageways were designed to cope with medieval traffic levels, but became increasingly inadequate for sixteenth- and seventeenth-century traffic. The consequence was that the houses on the bridges had to be demolished to increase the widths of the roadways, and eventually the bridges themselves had to be rebuilt. By the mid-eighteenth century the Bath bridge was therefore a highly unusual experiment.

The fields to which it gave access were part of the 600-acre manor of Bathwick, belonging to the enormously wealthy Pulteney family who, amongst much else, are said to have owned a *million* acres in and around New York. The Pulteneys were well aware of the potential value of their Bathwick estate, and had first considered building a bridge in 1757. William Johnstone Pulteney revived the idea in 1767 when he saw an opportunity to do a deal with the City Corporation. Bath had not only outgrown its supply of building land, but its water supply as well. He had both.

He was a Scottish lawyer who had been born William Johnstone, and had taken his hugely wealthy wife's name on his marriage. Her fortune derived from her rich father (who had the distinction of being Prime Minister for one day) and even richer mother (who had the distinction of being a beauty whose accommodating attitude to her many admirers caused her to be known as Mrs Pony). William Johnstone Pulteney was in a highly fortunate but slightly constricted position. The land was entailed, so his wife only held a life interest in it, and having no sons, on her death it would pass to their daughter, Henrietta Laura Pulteney,[1] the income meanwhile remaining with her father during his lifetime. Although he couldn't make decisions about the land unless he first got the trustees' approval, it appears that he usually did. In 1769 he persuaded them to let him build the bridge, arguing that it would make the land developable.

He then immediately made an agreement to supply Bath with water from his springs on Bathwick Down in return for the Corporation doing two things: transferring land on the city side of the river so that he could clear an approach road, and agreeing to obtain the necessary Act of Parliament. They got their Act in 1769, which gave them the compulsory purchase powers to clear the site, but stipulated that the bridge had to be free of tolls. Pulteney then commissioned Thomas Paty of Bristol, who had recently built (to somebody else's design) the new Bristol Bridge, to design and build his bridge. When it was half complete, for some unknown reason he changed his mind and asked Adam to make a new design. Adam had been at Edinburgh University with him, was almost exactly the same age, and remained a lifelong friend. (Pulteney was one of the pallbearers at his funeral, the only plain mister, the others being a duke and four lords – how many architects could equal that?)

After some fairly disastrous technical problems, almost certainly due to Paty's foundations being designed for a much lighter and narrower bridge, work was completed in 1773 and the first shopkeepers moved in. (79) Pulteney Bridge, as it became known, was superb architecture, vastly superior to the North Bridge in Edinburgh which had been finished three years earlier, but after all the necessary rebuilding much more expensive. The Edinburgh bridge cost £14 per linear foot, the Bath one £59.

Like so many Adam compositions, for example the sides of Fitzroy and Charlotte Squares in London, the bridge had central and end pavilions where the central one repeated the overall composition in miniature, i.e. it consisted of central and end pavilions itself. The true end pavilions were tiny domed buildings with a pediment on all four sides, each originally with flat-topped toy porticos, with their Doric columns seeming to stand on tip-toe on their pedestals. (80) Apart from the few columns and pilasters there was no other ornament, not even the usual triglyphs and metopes in the frieze.[2] The internal elevation facing the street was equally simple, with the same articulation of small pavilions, and with each shop front and a tiny first-floor window contained within an arch. It is perhaps legitimate to make a very small practical criticism of Adam's design. As it stands today in the middle of a built-up area it is possible to cross the bridge, especially from east to west, without realising that one is on a bridge at all and that there is a river beneath one's feet. On the centre span of the Ponte Vecchio there is a gap in the shops so that one can lean on the parapet and admire the view or play Pooh sticks. It was unlike Robert Adam to miss an opportunity like that, but providing it would have cost a shop on either side.

1 In 1996 the Holburne Museum acquired a bewitching full length portrait of the 11-year-old Henrietta Laura Pulteney by Angelica Kauffmann.

2 One of the more curious rules of classical composition was that triglyphs and metopes could be omitted if required. As we saw in chapter 3, when they were used they were an extremely tyrannical constraint upon the positioning of doors, windows and columns. This difficulty was a challenge that most architects enjoyed accepting. No doubt Adam omitted them on the bridge to save money, but also because he didn't want the rather gloomy solemnity they give.

79 Pulteney Bridge.
Robert Adam, 1773.
Engraving after Thomas
Malton. (Image from
Bath in Time)

80 Pulteney Bridge, the
entrance from the city.
Aquatint by Thomas
Malton. (Image from
Bath in Time)

THE CLASSICAL BUILDINGS OF BATH

81 Pulteney Bridge today

No sooner was the bridge completed than the outbreak of the American War of Independence caused a financial crisis which stopped speculative house building, so for a number of years the bridge led only to fields and a few scattered houses. In 1788 work began at last on the building of roads and houses. Understandably, during those years when the bridge led to nowhere in particular it had been very difficult to find tenants for all the shops on it. In 1792, when house building was under way, a tenant agreed to take most of them, but required massive changes which involved converting the sixteen shops into six larger ones, raising their roofs, demolishing the porticos at the west end and numerous consequent minor alterations. From then, until the 1940s, change after change took place until the bridge became the travesty of Adam's design which we see today.

Two alterations are particularly disastrous. One is the shortening of the west half of the bridge. It is not immediately apparent because when it was done the western end pavilion was moved eastwards, but it has left the bridge grotesquely asymmetrical, which is made worse by the fact that several windows have been blocked. (81) The other disastrous alteration is the removal of the pair of tiny porticos that greeted people about to cross the bridge from either end. It would be enormously difficult and costly to restore the bridge to its original condition, and maybe impossible, but the Corporation in recent years has gone some way towards that.

The famous view of the bridge is the one from the south, with the Avon flowing over its weir in front, but the north face has its own fascination. (82) It is an incredibly ramshackle and picturesque collection of clipped-on sheds hanging precariously from the structure, added over the years by shopkeepers desperate to obtain more space. In 1900 the south front was going the same way, but the Corporation has cleared the clutter on that side and recently improved its internal shop frontage. It would be pleasant if the north side could be preserved in its present picturesque condition, both as a reminder of the period when the pendulum of taste made Adam's work contemptible, and in its own right as a remarkable incident in Bath's townscape.

During the financial crisis Pulteney had to erect one building immediately. This was because the necessary road clearance on the Bath side of the river had required the demolition of St Mary's church, long used as the city's prison, and he had agreed to build a bigger replacement on his own land. It was built in 1772 to the design of Thomas Atwood. (83) It is a handsome and remarkably benign structure, looking more like a large house than a prison, and nothing like George Dance's deliberately grim and horrifying Newgate in London, which was under construction at the same time. No doubt the reason for the Bath version's reassuring appearance was that as soon as house building started again it would be a near neighbour to people who would not want to be reminded of the more unpleasant facts of urban life. Today it looks

83 The Prison. Thomas Atwood, 1752. The exposure of the originally hidden basement storey has upset the façade's finely judged proportions

slightly ridiculous and its lovely proportions are spoilt because the basement, originally unseen below street level, was exposed to view when the street was lowered in the nineteenth century. When this was done the entrance porch was converted into a window and a new door opened at the lower level. To appreciate the building now one must imagine it without the basement. The design, with its rusticated ground floor and slightly projecting ends, looks earlier than its date, more like work of the Palladian 1740s.

Pulteney meanwhile was preparing his wife's land for development. When leases fell in he renewed them only on an annual basis, and two or three years after the bridge's completion he went back to Adam and asked him to draw up a layout for developing the land as a new town – Bathwick. By then he had conceived the idea of building a second bridge, this time at Bathford, and a turnpike road linking the two. This would have short-cut the Walcot turnpike and diverted all the London traffic through his land. Hardly surprisingly there was an uproar. Earlier, when he had changed his bridge plans and added shops, without any authority for doing so in the Act of Parliament, the Corporation had protested. On that occasion he had managed to calm everybody down, this time he failed and had to drop the idea, though in 1774 he had another go, which was equally unsuccessful. Adam prepared several alternative street plans and some brilliant elevations, submitting the first scheme to Pulteney in June 1777 and a final version in 1782. Since they were not carried into reality they are a footnote in the history of town planning rather than the concern of a history of classical Bath, but they are interesting to us for a couple of reasons.

The first is Adam's rejection of the ideas in Craig's Edinburgh plan, then making its slow progress westward. It was much the most obvious potential prototype since the two projects were not only contemporary with each other but were intended for the same thing – long streets of substantial houses. The most striking aspect of Adam's Bath layouts is that they look as though they were designed to be as different from Craig's rather pedestrian plan as possible. Their second point of interest is that they clearly pay homage to John Wood, since they employ both the circus and crescent forms, neither of which appear in Craig's plan (though both were used in the later extensions to it). For some unknown reason, in or around 1782 Pulteney decided not to go ahead with Adam's plans and instead instructed Thomas Baldwin to draw alternatives. In 1789 he accepted them and instructed him to go ahead with building. The most likely explanation for the change is the series of problems that arose during construction of the bridge, and their disastrous effect on its cost. Pulteney probably thought that for his Bathwick streets he needed an architect on the spot rather than one based in distant London and working all over the country. Whatever the explanation, he kept his friendship with Adam.

So, for reasons we can't know for certain, Adam's direct involvement in Bath's development closed, though his influence lived on. Among the many fine architects and urban planners that the City of Bath has produced, Thomas Baldwin (1750-1820) is second only to the elder John Wood in both capacities. He was not a genius and he was not an innovator, but a follower of Chambers, and to a lesser extent Adam, though by no means slavishly in either case. He designed one or two dud buildings, but several which are extremely beautiful. Although his planning of Great Pulteney Street and Laura Place has been much lauded, his brilliant transformation of central Bath has rarely had the understanding it deserves. It will be examined in the next chapter.

As we noted in the last chapter, the few years on either side of 1790 were one of those periods of boom with which we are so familiar in our own time, when it seems that every speculation must turn to gold. At first they all do and fortunes are made, encouraging even more dangerous speculations. But they always end with a bust. In the years 1789-93, throughout Britain a huge number of new houses were projected in every town that seemed to show a chance of growing. For decades not many towns had grown faster than Bath, so confidence was high and few towns saw such ambitious plans. During those four years the number of houses is said by Prof. Neale to have increased by 45%, coach services from London by 70%, and river traffic (bringing timber and other building materials) by more than 100%. Amongst the new houses were those in Bathwick New Town. In 1788, 14 years after the bridge was completed, Pulteney's daughter, Henrietta Laura Pulteney, began letting 99-year leases to speculating builders. As was by then normal, the leases bound them to adhere to elevations that Baldwin had designed. Thereafter things went quickly for a few years. The first short stretch of road after the bridge is called Argyle Street, it then comes to a diamond-shaped space called Laura Place and continues as Great Pulteney Street. Two other roads, Henrietta Street and Johnstone Street, go off Laura Place, making it one of the grandest cross-roads in the country. The first stone in Laura Place was laid in March 1788.

Baldwin didn't want a simple cross-roads, he wanted a *place*[3], a pause before his great street. That meant he had to open out the space. It had to provide a junction between the relatively narrow Argyle, Johnstone and Henrietta Streets and the much wider Great Pulteney Street, and in order to make any impact it had to be considerably wider than any of them. One of Adam's plans for the area had had a circus at about this point, another of them had an oval. With roads as wide as Adam was contemplating a circus was a bad idea: it would have been much gap and little enclosure. An oval was better because it allowed more room for the enclosing houses. Baldwin must have played with the idea, but he rejected it, probably because walling built on a relatively small radius is too expensive for speculative houses, and to have had a facetted 'curve', made up of the flat house fronts set at a slight angle to each other, he would have had to mask the junctions in some way, perhaps as Wood had done at the Circus and the Crescent, which would have introduced further expense. So he had to have a flat-sided shape. He had two options. The first, the standard solution, was to plan the *place* at right angles to the axis, with each road entering in the middle of a side. He chose the second, less usual, option. He planned a diamond-shaped *place* at an angle to the axis, with the roads coming in at the corners. That gave him a tricky geometrical problem because Great Pulteney Street was wider than the others. If he planned each of the sides at the same angle they would be of unequal length, which would produce an informal space, the last quality he was looking for. So, since all four enclosing terraces had to be of equal length, they had to be at different angles. The opposite sides are therefore not parallel to each other. On a plan that looks awkward, but in reality it is of no visual consequence, and in a way is an advantage because it makes the space less obvious and more interesting.

3 As I have mentioned earlier in this book, the English language is deficient in this respect. Because we have no word to describe an open urban space unless it is square, triangular or circular I use the French word *place*.

84 Laura Place. Thomas Baldwin, 1788

THE CLASSICAL BUILDINGS OF BATH

Having arrived at a shape that gave him four terraces of equal length, Baldwin had to decide on their height. By then he must have decided, on aesthetic grounds, that since the entire site is flat the parapet level in Great Pulteney Street was to run right through from end to end; and, almost certainly on commercial grounds, that all the houses were to be of three fairly lofty storeys, plus garrets and basements.[4] He decided to maintain this pattern in Laura Place, as his new space was called, though some architects would have wanted to make them higher to provide variety and a climax, as Nash did a few years later in London in Regent (now Piccadilly) Circus. Baldwin also maintained the same parapet and other horizontal lines in Johnstone and Henrietta Streets. This produces an effect which some people have found monotonous, especially as the articulating elements – the pilasters, pediments and so on – are very weak and unemphatic. But it has a major compensating virtue: it produces remarkably calm and stately streets.

Each of the Laura Place terraces consists of three houses and one bay of another at each end, the rest of which is around the corner. (84) In each terrace the central house has five bays, with its middle first-floor window emphasised. The flanking houses are narrower, of three bays, with their central windows emphasised, but less strongly. Overall, the proportion of length to height is very satisfying. But few people ever look at one of the façades by itself, they see them as part of the whole *place*. Baldwin's great achievement in Laura Place is the successful way in which he makes a unity of the four buildings, the four gaps, and the area between them. Architecturally it is potentially one of the most attractive open spaces in Bath, but today it is almost impossible to appreciate its beauty because it is now dominated by parked cars, tarmac and clutter. For its first century of life the more attractive un-tarmaced road surface was narrower, the pavements wider, and parking restricted to an occasional waiting carriage.

Throughout Great Pulteney Street Baldwin used exactly the same decorative details he had used in Laura Place, including the fluted Corinthian pilasters running through the first and second floors. (85) In the short terraces of Laura Place they do their job very well, but in the much longer Great Pulteney Street they become tedious – if one notices them. One seldom does, they are of such slight projection, and spaced apart so sparingly, that they make scarcely any impression. When standing in the street it takes real effort to work out what is going on, even on the south

85 Great Pulteney Street. Over-thin and attenuated pilasters

4 In architectural nomenclature an attic is a storey above the entablature, with its outer walls a continuation in the same plane as those below. The upper floors of Cavendish Place and Crescent are examples. A garret is a storey in which the rooms are built within the roof.

86 Great Pulteney Street.
Pedimented pavilion
arranged to face down
Edward Street

side, which is the better of the two. There is a system, but it would be pointless to explain it because it is itself almost pointless. In only one respect does it work well, in being so arranged that each of the side roads is faced by one of the pavilions in Great Pulteney Street. (86) Apart from that the classical ordering is ineffectual. Baldwin was a highly skilled designer, so what is the explanation?

Almost certainly money: this was a much more expensive venture than meets the eye. That only becomes clear when one looks at the back of the houses from either the park on the north or the rugby ground on the south. The ground there is more than a storey lower than the road because the entire complex, houses and road, has been lifted up onto a raised platform. In other words, the basement floors are a little above natural ground level, and the road and entrance floors are a storey above ground. (Some of the houses even have cellars below their basements.) The reason, of course, was the danger of flooding on these riverside meadows. The leases required the lowest floors to be 2ft above 'the highest flood mark on John Warren's mill'. Baldwin had two alternatives, either to build the road at basement level and the pavement a storey above it (as in several Bath streets such as Walcot Parade and Belmont) or, much more expensively, raise the road up a storey. The cheaper solution would have had the merit of allowing service deliveries from wheeled vehicles to be at the level of the kitchen and other service rooms, which would have been convenient for the servants but of no direct advantage to their employers. Indeed, it would have been of some slight disadvantage to them and their visitors since it would have given them additional steps to negotiate when entering or leaving their carriages. But the more convenient and expensive solution, the elevated road, had a huge visual advantage, it produced a much simpler, broader, and handsomer street scene. In order to afford that great aesthetic advantage, Baldwin had to keep his façades as cheap, and therefore as simple, as possible. Despite its defects the street is glorious. The classical apparatus is almost superfluous – needed to give the necessary social tone, but having little other significance. Baldwin relied on noble proportions and princely dimensions to make his point.

Several builders worked on the street, each undertaking a varying number of houses. Things began very slowly. In 1784 only one house was built, in '85 only one again, and the following year none at all. Then in 1787 when the boom began, six were completed, and thereafter in the five years until the end of '92, an average of 21 each year. That came to a sudden end when, on February 1st 1793, the French Convention declared war on Britain. There was an almost immediate financial panic, and in March a disastrous collapse. In that year not a single house was completed. Everybody who was owed money, or had money in a bank, wanted to get their hands on it, and everybody suddenly became slower at paying their bills – if they paid them at all. The builders of Great Pulteney Street and other developments in Bath were financed by loans from the local banks. In 1793 two of the banks became bankrupt, including the Bath City Bank which was funding the Great Pulteney Street builders. Inevitably Baldwin and other builders and craftsmen followed, leaving a rag-bag of people to finish the work they left uncompleted. Baldwin lived for many more years, continuing in a rather desultory way to work as an architect, but his career in Bath was effectively over. Whilst he worked there he had given the city more than any other architect had done since Wood, not only at Bathwick, but in his equally important improvements to the central area of the city, which are described in the next chapter.

So Pulteney Street was a disaster for almost everybody involved. But not quite everybody: when Pulteney's wife inherited the estate in 1767 it had produced an income of £735 pa. By 1817, when development was virtually complete, the figure was £18,932. (At today's value the figure would be around £800,000).

In addition to its glorious proportions, Pulteney Street owes a great deal to the termination at its east end. (87) At that point, where the ground starts to rise, Baldwin planned a great

hexagon of roads with houses facing onto a pleasure garden in the middle. This was to replace the Spring Gardens over part of which he had laid out Johnstone Street, but here on a much bigger scale. Pleasure gardens, with music, dancing and refreshments, and entry by ticket, were then all the rage, and despite the financial crisis, after a short pause Sydney Gardens were laid out and opened to the public in 1795, but to the design of Charles Harcourt Masters (1759-after 1820) who was a minor Bath architect and land surveyor who had survived the financial collapse.[5] To terminate the view looking up Great Pulteney Street, Baldwin had planned a fashionable new type of building, a hotel, to stand at the front of the Gardens so that it faced down the axis to Pulteney Bridge a third of a mile away. This also was built to a design by Harcourt Masters. Baldwin's design was for a relatively wide and low building, only two storeys high and thus lower than the houses leading up to it. We are unable to judge whether it would have been successful because as built by Harcourt Masters in 1796-7 the hotel was three storeys high, and in 1836 a fourth storey was added, very successfully, by the younger John Pinch. Finally, between 1913-16 Sir Reginald Blomfield converted it into the museum it is today. He gutted the interior, installed a grand marble staircase, blocked the second-floor windows to provide an exhibition gallery at that level, added the central parapet on the front and built the single-storey Doric screens on either side of the façade. The aesthetic price for this was that the rear elevation, previously the best, now became the worst, stripped of its main feature, the great semi-circular balcony on which, in the early years of

5 Today Sydney Gardens must be the only public park in Britain amongst whose most popular attractions are a main railway line and a canal.

the century, bands had played to the revellers in Sydney Gardens. It was a small price to pay: his façade and the great bank of trees behind it, make a superlative termination to Great Pulteney Street. In the late 1870s the city council planted trees in Great Pulteney Street, presumably rooted in pockets in the raised vault structure. Although they reached roof level, in all the photographs they look starved and were presumably removed either because they didn't flourish, or their roots were causing problems. Although they were quite widely spaced their effect on the appearance of the street was unfortunate, and would have been worse if they had grown more vigorously. Since their removal in about 1950 the trees behind the Holburne Museum have no competitors. Over the last few decades the council has greatly improved the appearance of the street by closing Pulteney Bridge to traffic, thereby substantially reducing the flow along Great Pulteney Street. If the parking in Laura Place could be removed the transformation would be almost complete. But one thing would still be missing. At the city end there is no visual termination equivalent to the Holburne Museum and the trees behind it. They are a complete barrier allowing no views beyond. That would be inappropriate at the city end: what is needed there is a partial stop, a tall slim vertical which would terminate the street but allow views beyond into the city. In 1877 there was an attempt to provide one when a tall fountain was built in Laura Place. It was ugly and of insufficient presence to be successful. In 1977 it was reduced to the present stump, a horribly appropriate companion to the parking meters and clutter. When, finally, the cars are removed from Laura Place, its paving will have to be re-designed and perhaps then a benefactor will commission something which will glorify the westward view down Great Pulteney Street and give Laura Place the central focus without which it will remain relatively formless.

88 By the closing decades of the 18th century the often dark and cramped entrance lobbies of earlier years had become unacceptable in the more expensive houses. Fanlight in Edward Street

The perfect proportions of Great Pulteney Street; the warm colour of the stone which, now it is clean, is like a solar battery, still seeming to reflect the sun on dull days, and changing from a pale oatmeal in a cool light to orange when the sun is setting; the Museum glowing at the end against its great bank of trees; the street's wonderful state of preservation and the absence of trees allowing the architecture to be seen properly; make it the most satisfying long classical street in Britain.

7 Transformation of the city centre

In the half century from 1750 to 1800 Bath's population grew from around seven thousand to thirty-three thousand, so accommodation in the city's relatively few churches became increasingly inadequate. The Church of England had effectively gone to sleep and its role of catering for the working population was being taken over by the Methodists and others. Prosperous families tended to remain faithful to the Established Church because they ran and staffed it, but even they were finding it difficult to buy pews in Bath. So private enterprise had to supply what ecclesiastical lethargy could not. We have seen how the building of John Wood's proprietory chapel just off Queen Square produced a handsome income and a crop of takers for his houses. In 1766 a Bath banker assembled a group of investors who built a proprietory chapel in the garden of his house on the east side of Milsom Street. Whether their motives were spiritual or pecuniary is not recorded. The chapel opened in the following year to the design of Timothy Lightoler (1727-69), a carver-joiner of Warwick who built a modestly successful architectural practice. He was a man of many gifts, author, engraver and patentee of a machine for cutting steel files. He was in practice with his brother who shared his mechanical interests: he augmented his income by coining. When arrested he escaped and fled the country. Timothy's only building in Bath, the Octagon Chapel, is a square windowless box getting all its

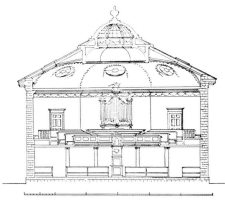

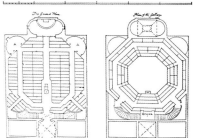

89 Octagon Chapel. Timothy Lightoler, 1767. 18th-century engraving. From Mowbray Green

daylight from above. (89) Internally the angles of the square are chamfered off to form an octagon, with semi-circular alcoves in the chamfers, two of which contain fireplaces. The sanctuary is a rectangle with semi-circular alcoves at either side. Above, a gallery encircles the room, and above that a huge octagonal cove supports a domed lantern. There are circular windows in each face of the great cove. A splendid organ originally stood above the sanctuary and became famous because of the fine organist, who was William Herschel the great astronomer who discovered Uranus. Throughout the remainder of the eighteenth century and part of the nineteenth the Octagon Chapel was the most fashionable church in Bath, but fashion is a fickle jade. By the middle of the nineteenth century the Chapel's almost rococo atmosphere was perceived as being frivolous and un-Christian. The congregation drifted away to the new repent-or-burn Gothic churches and the Chapel finally closed in 1895. Since then no permanent use has been found for it.

By the mid-eighteenth century Walcot, which contained nearly all the new houses, had the second largest population of any parish in England. Its tiny medieval parish church of St Swithin was grossly inadequate. Numerous demands that it should be rebuilt, and proposals for doing so, were ignored by the church until by the 1770s it could resist no longer. John Palmer and Thomas Jelly were appointed to rebuild it, and the new church was opened in 1777. Even that was half-hearted because only a few years later a further two bays had to be added to the original six. Finally, in 1790, the tower and spire were built. (90) The body of the church is a typical rectangular preaching box with galleries on three sides. The galleries are lit by high arched windows, the seating under them by smaller rectangular ones. Externally there is a giant Ionic pilaster between each window. The tower, with lobbies on either side of it, stands in front of the box. The lobbies have been subsequently given another storey cutting across the arched gallery windows, spoiling the entrance front of this otherwise decent design. The church, being classical, was unusual at this time, the other new churches in Bath were all Gothic, and therefore outside the scope of this book. Most are rather dull, but one or two, such as Wilson and Wilcox's St Paul's in Monmouth Street, are of real quality.

90 St Swithin's church. John Palmer and Thomas Jelly, 1777-1790

We must now examine Baldwin's work in the centre of the city. Although he was Bath's greatest architect after Wood, nothing is known of his early career. He was born in 1749 or 1750, and is first recorded in Bath in 1774. In the following year, at the age of 26, he built the Guildhall, a superb mature design, suggesting that he must have obtained a first-class professional training somewhere. At that time he was employed as Thomas Warr Atwood's clerk (what we would call an architectural assistant), but not much is known about that relationship. Atwood was a prosperous building tradesman and influential member of the Common Council, which position he used whenever he could to further his own business. This infuriated his competitors but was not considered at that time to be particularly unethical. At times he operated as an architect but it seems possible that all or most of his buildings were designed by members of his staff. There is no evidence that he had sufficient talent to have given Baldwin his training.

The city's old town hall, known as the Guildhall, was one of the countless second-rate seventeenth-century buildings throughout the country which were claimed to have been designed by Inigo Jones. By the mid-eighteenth century it had become far too small and inadequate, so in 1760 the Council resolved to replace it. A design prepared by Timothy Lightoler, and slightly later another by John Palmer, had been quashed and Atwood manoeuvred himself into the saddle. By July 1775 his Markets behind the Guildhall were under construction and his design for the Guildhall itself, almost certainly the work of his assistant

91 Guildhall.
Thomas Baldwin, 1788

THE CLASSICAL BUILDINGS OF BATH

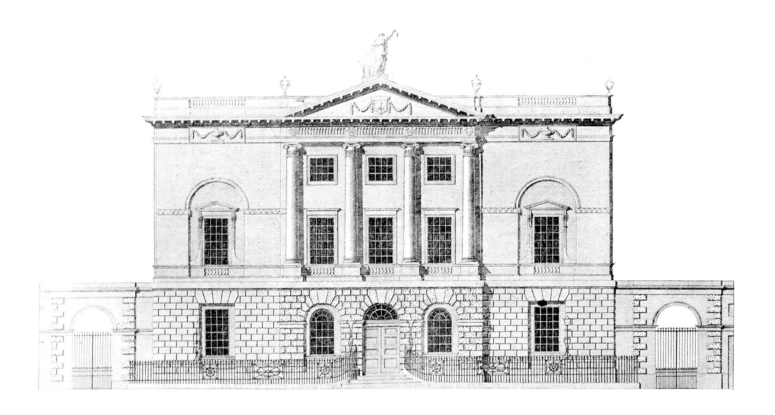

92 Guildhall. Engraving
from Mowbray Green

Baldwin, was accepted by the Corporation. A few months later, at the end of 1775, Atwood was killed when the floor of an old building he was examining, collapsed. The Council appointed Baldwin to proceed, and a month or two later to be the City Architect and Surveyor. Three years later he became Deputy Chamberlain as well, and in 1787 Inspector of the Baths.

His new Guildhall, one of the most serenely beautiful buildings in Bath, was completed in 1778. (91) Although the front elevation of the main block remains substantially intact, it has been mutilated by the loss of two tiny wings (which were screen walls fronting the markets), and by the building having been encased on each side by 1890s extensions. The contemporary engraving shows how much was lost by this. (92) The wings gave a broad base to a triangular composition which, with their removal, is now lost, and the extensions converted what had been a free-standing building into a mere façade which is simply an incident in a long line of later ones. In fact the extensions, when considered on their own, are of high quality, but their effect on Baldwin's façade was unfortunate. They will be discussed in chapter nine.

The ground floor is rusticated, and in the frontispiece enriched with vermiculation.[1] This is capped by a broad unmoulded platband on which stand the four unfluted Ionic columns supporting the pediment. All this is fairly routine late Palladian design, but carried out with a delicacy which is typical of its 1775 date, and revealing something of the influence of Robert

1 Stonework carved with little curved grooves thought to resemble worm-casts.

93 Guildhall, pediment

Adam and rather more of William Chambers. It is instructive to contrast the precision of this 1770s façade with the more ponderous details of earlier buildings such as the Assembly Rooms. There, there is nothing to equal the beautiful enriched Ionic capitals (93) or the subtle way in which the vertical formed by the two side windows set in their great arches is continued upwards by a tablet in the frieze containing a delicate festoon, and then up again to a row of balusters in the parapet. The unsympathetic dome was added in 1890 by J. M. Brydon when he built the long wings on either side.

94 Guildhall,
rear elevation

The back elevation is equally fine. (94) The ground floor is again rusticated, but instead of the front's single pedimented feature in the centre, here there are two of them, one at each end. The centre is emphasised by a pair of Corinthian pilasters framing the central window and supporting a delicate pediment. The windows in the second floor are oval bulls' eyes set in rectangular frames, except in the centre where there is a slightly smaller rectangular recess containing a carved festoon. Above and behind this is a chimney in the enchanting form of a small Roman altar (a great deal more beautiful than the real one at the Temple of Sulis Minerva).

The interior is no less delightful. A grand staircase with wrought-iron balustrading leads up to the two great rooms on the first floor. The smaller of the two was the Common Council's meeting chamber, and the larger was the sumptuous Banqueting Hall. (95) When reading contemporary accounts of seventeenth- and eighteenth-century town councils, one is left with the probably not entirely misleading impression that the councillors' main business was feasting and drinking at the public expense. Michael Forsyth fascinatingly points out that Bath's Guildhall could be regarded as a riposte to the Upper Assembly Rooms from which the civic dignitaries, being tradesmen, were socially excluded. The Banqueting Hall is superior to anything in the Assembly Rooms, but the proportions are still Palladian, with a length twice and a height three-quarters of the width (80ft x 40ft x 30ft). The decoration has usually been described as in Adam's style, but, as with the exterior, it is more influenced by Chambers. The magnificent chandeliers (which were chosen by Baldwin personally) are even better and more expensive than those in the Assembly Rooms, the fine portraits with their gilded frames are

integrated into the wall decoration, and the colours are livelier than those in the Assembly Rooms, making this a superb and memorable interior.

While the Guildhall was under construction, Baldwin indulged in a private speculation, the construction of Northumberland Buildings, a row of houses forming the south side of Wood Street, which is a continuation of the south side of Queen Square. (96) It was the first four-storey terrace in Bath, built only a few years after the Adams's four-storey Adelphi in London. Unfortunately Baldwin had not yet learnt how to cope with this new problem. Good Palladians such as the younger John Wood (who was 50 when it was built) must have felt that the old rules which had governed their work were vindicated, because the proportions of Northumberland Buildings are unpleasant – which is exactly what Palladian orthodoxy suggested they would be. The height is too great for the length, the top floor looks like a later addition, and the end and central pavilions are so weakly articulated that they make no impact whatever. For that reason they and their three pediments, which have no pilasters to draw attention to them, are lost in that huge façade. If the pediments are noticed at all they seem to be stuck onto the façade quite

96 Northumberland
Buildings. Thomas
Baldwin, 1788

arbitrarily. To be fair, the details are extremely elegant and the building has been badly treated since it was built: all the first-floor windows and many on the top floor have been elongated, most have had their reveals splayed and lost their glazing bars. If the building were to be given a thorough restoration it would doubtless look better, but it could never be more than a curiosity. It is something of an embarrassment to Baldwin's reputation.

He made up for it in his next row of houses, Somerset Buildings in Milsom Street, which were built a year or two later in 1782. (97) Despite what several authors have written to the contrary, it is superb, one of his finest designs: less adventurous than Northumberland Buildings but infinitely more successful architecturally. Whereas Northumberland Buildings is a cliff of four uncontrolled storeys, this is a little palace façade of three beautifully regulated storeys; where that is relatively flat, this is richly plastic. The two don't look like the work of the same man (until you study the small details, some of which in Northumberland Buildings are excellent).

When Daniel Milsom developed his street in the 1760s he was unable to acquire all the land

97 Somerset Buildings.
Thomas Baldwin, 1782

for his east side because it was occupied by the town's Poor House. In 1780 that was demolished and Baldwin obtained the building lease. Instead of squeezing-in a row of narrow houses like Milsom's, he built a terrace of five very grand ones, and instead of stepping them up one by one like the others, built them on the level so that their horizontal lines run through the five houses uninterruptedly. That enabled him to design them as a single formal composition on the conventional pattern of a rusticated base with arched windows and doors, and plain ashlar upper floors. Not much else is conventional. The 3-bay end houses are treated as pavilions with pediments supported on four fluted Corinthian columns, the 5-bay central house has no pediment, but instead has its three inner bays projected forward in a huge segmental bow.

All the first-floor windows have a blind balustrade and the three inner houses have a balustraded parapet.

The design of the central house (i.e. the central pavilion) is particularly fascinating. (98) It would have been usual for the bow to have been articulated by four columns like the end pavilions, but here there is an additional one on the flat wall on either side of the bow. This is a clear example of influence from James Adam's Portland Place in London, probably from its derivative, the central house on the north side of Bedford Square, which is stuccoed to stand out from the brickwork of the houses on either side. The stucco extends for one bay on each side of pilastered and pedimented centre, thus widening it without the expense of additional pilasters. Baldwin's additional columns do exactly the same thing, but a great deal more expensively. The bay window and its rich dressing of columns is an extremely valuable urban feature because it projects just far enough into the street to be visible to people looking up or down it. Combined with the shallower end bays it gives Milsom Street much of its architectural vitality.

Most of the rest of it comes from Baldwin's other work in Milsom Street, which dates from the same years. (99) A few doors down from Somerset Buildings, on the corner with Green Street, he built a large five-bay single house employing the same basic pattern as his others, but using the Ionic

98 Somerset Buildings, the central pavilion

order instead of the Corinthian. The central bay projects very slightly and is crowned by a small pediment. Like Somerset Buildings there is a heavy cornice over the second-floor windows, but unlike them, there is an attic storey. The height of the windows decreases at each level as Palladio advised. The result is an extraordinarily beautiful Palladian façade, though the carved string course over the first-floor windows and the decorations in the Ionic frieze reveal its 1780s date. In some ways this is the most perfect small Palladian façade in Bath. It soon lost its perfection, when it was converted into a bank only a few years after it was completed, and, as with all the houses in the street, including Somerset Buildings, shopfronts were smashed into its ground floor. In the early years of the twentieth century, when eighteenth-century architecture

99 House on the corner of Milsom and Green Streets. Thomas Baldwin, 1780s. The sympathetic entrance was designed in 1908 by Herbert Matthews when he removed the 19th-century shopfronts

100 The Hot Bath, John
Wood the younger,
1775

was again appreciated after the usual period of rejection, that sort of vandalism came to be seen as offensive. It was the period when the first book on *The Eighteenth Century Architecture of Bath* was published, by the Bath architect Mowbray Green in 1904. Four years later another Bath architect, Herbert Matthews, restored the bank's ground floor, though the doorway and remarkably discreet curved name panel over it must be his design rather than Baldwin's.[2]

Somerset Buildings were not so lucky and had to wait longer for restoration, but slowly over the twentieth century most of the damage was put right. Today only one horribly intrusive terracotta ground floor remains. Let us hope that this century will secure its removal. Somerset Buildings has been illustrated in all the books on Bath's architecture since Mowbray Green's pioneering work, but it is an extraordinary fact that, as far as I am aware, until now no photograph of the glorious bank façade has ever been published in the books on Bath's architecture.

In 1785, Baldwin, this time acting as City Architect and using the Corporation's money, was instructed to prepare plans for a series of improvements in and around the ancient hot baths. All three of them were ramshackle and shapeless from centuries of alterations and rebuildings, dispersed at apparent random in a tangle of lanes. They were what drew all the visitors to Bath, but neither they nor their approaches had any of the order and urbanity for which the city was famous. The Corporation, which had owned them since the dissolution of the Abbey in the sixteenth century, had started the process of renewal ten years earlier in 1775 by commissioning the younger John Wood to rebuild the Hot Bath. (100) The plan of his interior

2 Michael Forsyth has established that the bank's return elevation in Green Street replaced a gabled house: the ground floor in 1930 and the upper floors in 1959

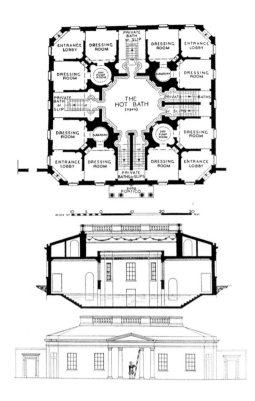

101 The Hot Bath, plan, section and front elevation. From Ison

was highly ingenious and attractive (101) but it was greatly altered in 1927. It contained eight very comfortable dressing rooms with fireplaces and ample room for the bather and a servant. The rooms were entered from four spacious lobbies at each chamfered corner of the building. Two pairs of the dressing rooms shared a tiny circular dry pump room, and two pairs shared an even smaller circular sudatory, presumably a sweating room utilising the spring's extremely hot water. The open-air pool in the centre of the building was a complex octagon, the water being entered from six stepped slips. The younger Wood's interiors at the Assembly Rooms show some skill at planning a sequence of differently shaped great rooms, but his relatively tiny interiors at the Hot Bath took that skill to a higher level. With this ability it is extraordinary that he was never able to plan a comparably attractive layout of buildings and streets, or indeed, to design any exteriors with more than a decent level of attractiveness. The exterior of the Hot Bath was, of course, a difficult design problem because none of the rooms were large enough to justify giving them, and therefore the building, any height. His decision to have four equally important entrances, one at each corner, should have meant that he couldn't have the usual portico. He simply ignored the logic and built one on the front of the building, no doubt justifying it by persuading himself – and surely us – that a portico need not be an entrance but could be a shelter for something. The something here was a small public pump and basin. (In 1927 the present door was substituted for the pump.) Externally the building is no more than modestly attractive. No doubt it looked better when it was an island of classical serenity in a jumble of sixteenth- and seventeenth-century clutter. Its rebuilding, however, made the other baths seem even shabbier by comparison, but the Corporation did nothing further for a decade.

At last, in 1784 the Council instructed Baldwin to add a tiny pump room to the ancient Cross Bath just across the road from the Hot Bath, and two years later to rebuild the Cross Bath itself. (It had got its name centuries earlier from a medieval cross which was removed in the sixteenth century.) In designing it Baldwin had to face the problem which had defeated Wood: the bath and its rooms were too small to justify giving them any height. He decided that if it couldn't be tall it could have a powerful personality instead: a sort of architectural Napoleon. (102) The main elevation has a double-curved front, more like a contemporary serpentine chest of drawers than any other English building one can think of. He even managed to achieve a respectable height by putting a short parapet in the centre of the façade, and on top of that a little turret holding a vase in a niche (a vase having a more relevant symbolism here than in most places where it was used in the eighteenth century). The result is one of the most beautiful small façades in the city.[3] Nothing could better illustrate the difference between the work of a decent and that of a brilliant architect than these two little Baths facing each other across the street. In 1785 Baldwin had been given instructions to plan improvements to the surrounding streets. When

3 Something similar is the exquisite entrance added at some unknown date to the flank wall of 1 Belmont where it turns into Hay Hill. It is a very intelligent paraphrase of Baldwin's Cross Bath façade, and if it wasn't designed by him it was the work of somebody who appreciated and understood his work there.

in the following year he built the Cross Bath, he had clearly not yet conceived the idea of Bath Street, because his building was not designed to face down it axially. That was put right in 1798 when John Palmer reconstructed the building and moved Baldwin's main front from the north to the east so that it formed Bath Street's glorious western termination. (103)

The Council was becoming increasingly worried that the number of visitors to the City was decreasing. The Season at Bath was no longer so essential a part of fashionable society's yearly round. The Councillors recognised that the squalid condition of the baths, and the disparity between the tangled and decaying medieval part of the town and the spacious modern developments to its north, was a discouragement to prospective visitors. Baldwin was instructed to draw a plan to show which existing streets should be widened, how communication between the Upper and Lower Town could be improved, and how the baths could be fitted more suitably into the fabric of the city. At the end of 1787 he produced his plan and was instructed to refine it in detail, prepare estimates of the cost of compulsorily acquiring the necessary properties, the cost of carrying out the huge reconstruction, and, finally, to produce estimates of the consequent increase in values to justify all this investment.

102 The Cross Bath.
   Thomas Baldwin, 1784.
   Re-oriented in 1798 by
   John Palmer so that its
   main front could face
   up Bath Street

103 Along Bath Street to the Cross Bath

The first part of this great programme was the construction of a New Private Bath in Stall Street, which Baldwin built in 1788. Its original interior no longer exists but its elevation onto Stall Street has survived much subsequent alteration and rebuilding. (104) Like the Hot and Cross Baths it is single storey, in this instance consisting of a long wall with its doors and niches separated by attached Ionic columns. The central four columns support a pediment with ornament designed in a pure Adam style: two sphinxes facing an oval wreath in which are a head of Hygeia and the sacred serpent of Aesculapius drinking from a cup. The symbolism of the sphinxes is obscure but the rest is ingenious and today (though not then) pleasantly recondite. On its own it is a very pleasant little façade, but it was soon to be part of a superlative architectural composition.

In 1790 Baldwin was instructed to demolish the old 1706 Pump Room facing onto the Abbey Churchyard, which, despite having been extended as recently as 1751, was universally recognised as being inadequate. He was then told to build a new one on a much grander scale. He designed it so that its western end elevation abutted and continued the line of his New Private Bath. The precise sequence of subsequent events is hard to follow but it is clear that the design of the north elevation and the interior were altered by John Palmer, who took over after Baldwin's dismissal (for which see later). The west elevation is almost certainly Baldwin's unaltered design.

The north façade facing onto the Abbey Churchyard is a failure, presumably because it is a jumble of both men's ideas. (105) It is known that Baldwin intended it to have a large project-ing Corinthian portico, of which the foundations were certainly built because they were revealed during work in the 1980s. There are indications that he had learnt the lesson of his Northumberland Buildings and intended the portico to reach the full height of the building so that its pediment could be in its proper place on the roof. Presumably under instructions to save money, Palmer changed this to the present arrangement where the columns are not free-standing or tall enough, and the pediment is lost way below the roof line. The huge side arches must be remnants of Baldwin's design because they are grotesquely out of scale with the present portico, but would have been ideal for a larger one. The row of oval windows are also probably Baldwin's, who used them on the Guildhall, but as used here threading through the portico's columns, are awkward (though they make a splendid effect internally). It is hard not to laugh at

the earnest inscription under the pediment which says Water is Best and somehow makes this clumsy façade look like a Victorian chapel. At least the numerous wealthy brewers who were trying to get into good society at that time would not have been offended: the message was veiled from them in gentlemanly Greek.

The worst feature of the north façade is its relationship with the west one, on Stall Street. If it were not for the parapet and the crowning entablature that run around both of them, there would be no relationship at all. None of the other horizontal lines run through, and though both fronts have giant Corinthian half-columns, they are of different sizes and stand at different heights. This makes the building, when seen in a three-quarter view, look extremely gauche, but fortunately few people notice it because it occurs at the point where the much more interesting colonnade diverts attention from it. Baldwin's Stall Street front, however, is magnificent. (106) It might be called abstract architecture since not one of its elements has a practical function. There are no windows and no doors, everything is designed purely to dress up the wall. It is architecture for architecture's sake, or putting that another way, it is architecture

104 Façade of the New Private Bath in Stall Street, now the entrance to the Roman Baths. Thomas Baldwin, 1788

105 Pump Room. John Palmer's botch-up of Thomas Baldwin's design

for the city's sake – civic design at its best. It stands tall on its high rusticated and vermiculated base, with three niches above framed by four pairs of engaged Corinthian columns.

The Abbey Churchyard had been a paved space for centuries, and was enclosed by houses. Old maps indicate that those on its west end were demolished at some time between 1776 and 1786, thus opening the space to Stall Street. Clearly Baldwin felt the need to re-enclose it visually, so he persuaded the Corporation to let him build a colonnade across it, exactly matching the one

106 Pump Room, Thomas Baldwin's Stall Street elevation

attached to the New Private Bath except that the columns in this one are made free-standing and not attached to a wall. It has the magical effect of simultaneously enclosing the space and exposing it. That sort of magic is a hard trick to pull off, and there has been unanimous praise ever since for the skill with which he did it. (107) A single row of columns wouldn't have worked so well because it would have been too insubstantial and transparent. Baldwin chose to have two rows of columns supporting a roof: in other words an open, transparent, building. Since the site falls gently towards the south and entablatures mustn't slope (as demonstrated by those of the

107 The double colonnade
  screening Abbey
  Churchyard from
  Stall Street. Thomas
  Baldwin, 1791

dreadful John Eveleigh), orthodoxy dictated that all the columns should be of the same height and the difference in levels made up by sitting them on a low wall or on individual pedestals or blocks. The wall was impossible because it would have acted as a barrier to movement. No doubt he tried out the pedestals on a drawing and disliked the way they coarsened his extremely delicate design. So he simply made all the columns of slightly different lengths. If either of the Woods had been around to see it they would have needed a long draught from the cup of Dionysos. Nothing shows more clearly how architectural times had changed; and changed surely for the better. It would be hard to deny that the illicit detail looks hugely better than the lawful one would have done. Baldwin could get away with this – as Robert Adam always did with his innovations – because he was a clever and sensitive designer. Eveleigh could not get away with his transgressions because they are an offence to the eye and not merely to the rule book.

When everything was finished Baldwin had therefore built an extremely beautiful symmetrical façade facing onto Stall Street which consisted of the tall end wall of the Pump Room, with a colonnade on either side of it, the one to the north open so that people could see and

108 Stall Street.
Thomas Baldwin's
Pump Room flanked
by his screens

walk through it, the one to the south closed by the wall of the New Private Baths. By any standards, this is the work of a master. (108) But he had done more than that. He had designed the façade of the Private Bath so that it was centred on an axis going off at a right angle to the Cross Bath, still hidden from view by the jumble of old houses along White Hart Lane. He was looking ahead, as John Wood junior could never do.

While work was continuing on the Pump Room and Private Baths he presented his plans and estimates for street improvements to the Corporation, three years after being instructed to do so. Presumably the reason they took so long to prepare, when he had obviously got them fairly clear in his mind before receiving his instructions, was that in addition to preparing the designs he had to negotiate valuations with cooperative property owners and make guesses about the likely cost of compulsorily buying the uncooperative ones, as well as preparing estimates of the cost of the new works. He finally proposed the demolition of a site that even today would be considered large and was then huge. The estimated cost of the properties to be bought was £47,163 (getting on for four million today), an enormous sum for an eighteenth-century town council to contemplate, when this sort of exercise was much less common than today. In March 1788 his plans and estimates were approved. Moves to obtain the necessary parliamentary authority were started, and the Bath Improvement Bill became an Act in 1789.[4] It gave the Corporation compulsory purchase powers, and power to enter properties to make

4 This was the Act which also authorised the building of Pulteney Bridge.

surveys. There then followed the process of buying up the old houses and clearing the site, which took another three years, being completed in 1791.

The Improvement Commissioners appointed by the Act worked quickly. In 1789, at their second meeting, Baldwin presented plans for widening Cheap Street and part of Stall Street, and at the next he was instructed to go ahead with Cheap Street. At the end of the year he was instructed to prepare designs for Bath Street (then called Cross Bath Street). Building work began in March 1791.

Stall Street, then so narrow that we would consider it little better than a lane, was widened by extending its width westwards onto the newly cleared site. Union Street was created, which is Stall Street's continuation to the north; Cheap and Westgate Streets were widened; and Bath Street was created – the link between the Cross and New Private Baths. At both ends of Bath Street Baldwin opened it out into the segment of a circle, making a little *place* with a curved side facing the Cross Bath at its west end, and another facing the New Private Baths at its east end.

This re-planning did a great deal more than connect up the baths and give them a formal setting: it totally transformed the central city. Previously the links between the north and south were dreadful, since the only connection between the Baths and Milsom Street, which was the way to Lansdown where most of the fashionable visitors stayed, was through the yard of an inn. This was replaced by the wide and elegant Union Street. Links between east and west had always been better, but the widening of Westgate and Cheap Streets, which crossed the north-south axis at a right angle, improved them and greatly increased the fashionable shopping area. For Cheap Street Baldwin designed terraces of plain-fronted houses on either side, with delightful bowed shop fronts on the nearly all-glass ground floors – a typically elegant late-eighteenth-century work anticipating the slightly later Regency. Unfortunately none of these enchanting shopfronts remain. The widening of Stall Street and the building of Bath Street provided yet more rows of fashionable shops, and more lodgings for visitors over them. In addition the Great Pump Room could now accommodate all the visitors to the spa in comfort and splendour; the King's Bath had been transformed and the New Private Baths built. These were the practical results of this huge civic enterprise, but the aesthetic gain, in a city whose success was largely based on its reputation for beauty, was much greater. The formalising of Abbey Churchyard, its subtle linking with newly beautified Stall Street, and the stunning sequence from there along Bath Street, had taken the city into the forefront of urban design in Britain once again.

Baldwin obviously wanted his new Bath Street to be a formal promenade between the baths, but it had to accommodate shops whose rents were essential to its financial success. Because some shopkeepers will always try to shout each other down, shops and architectural formality are uneasy bedfellows. Like Inigo Jones before and John Nash after him, Baldwin saw that the only way to maintain a properly formal parade and absorb any shopkeeper's over-exuberance was to recess the shops behind colonnades. This had the additional advantage of allowing people in wet weather to shop or to walk between the baths and the Pump Room under cover. He again chose the Ionic order he had used at his two Stall Street colonnades. On the upper floors he emphasised the strongly horizontal character established by the colonnade by having a wide cill band carved with his favourite running scroll motif. (109) (The Bath masons, or more probably their apprentices, would have been able to run off this scroll almost automatically. There are hundreds of metres of it in the city, all carved within a few years.) On the first floor the individuality of each house is expressed by giving its central window a pediment supported on console brackets, lifted above the top of the window to allow space for a couple of Adamesque swags. Apart from the columns, the scrolled cill band and these windows, there is no other ornament. (110)

109 Bath Street.
Second-floor cill band

It seems surprising that in rainy Britain putting pavements under cover has rarely been popular. Inigo Jones's versions in Covent Garden were disliked because they became the haunt of prostitutes at night and men with urgent bladders at all times. Nash's versions in Regent Street were so unpopular for the same reasons that they, like Inigo's, were eventually removed. In fact it is probable that the main reason was not the activities of whores, but that not being subject to the natural washing of rain the pavements had to be cleaned each morning by the shopkeepers. There is no evidence of what persuaded Baldwin and his client to try again where Covent Garden had failed, but a contemporary example in Paris seems highly likely to have been the spur. As we have seen, he must have planned the line of the street in about 1785 or '86. His proposals and estimates were accepted in 1788, so his decision to put the shops behind a colonnade was almost certainly made between those years. A few years earlier than that, between 1781 and 1783, the garden of the Palais-Royal in Paris had been enclosed by new buildings forming a very large courtyard, and in 1784 had opened to the public with rows of 'English' shops under vaulted colonnades. It rapidly became the most popular and fashionable shopping centre in France, drawing people from all over Europe to see it (including Mrs Thrale, a regular visitor to Bath and later a resident in the city). Its fame was so widespread that many other people in Bath at the time would have known about it. It was much bigger than Bath Street, and its architectural treatment (by Victor Louis, not at his best) was quite different, the elevations being crowded with pilasters and ornament – not at all English. But the idea was identical. That was not all. Running across the Palais-Royal's Great Court was a screen of two rows of columns supporting a roof, like Baldwin's version, but larger. It would be a remarkable coincidence if the Palais-Royal had nothing to do with Bath Council's decision to ignore the fact that covered pavements had never been successful in Britain, and to allow Baldwin to put the shops in Bath Street under cover and build his expensive and beautiful, but practically useless, screen between Abbey Churchyard and Stall Street.

For more than a century the Bath Street shops prospered while people were passing up and down on their way to the baths, but in the first half of the twentieth century when the baths languished they languished also, and in the second half most of them closed. The reason was that by then Bath Street led nowhere. (It is a recognised fact of shop design that if shops are in a cul-de-sac there must be some powerful draw at the end of it: today, for example, a major supermarket.) The empty shops and in some cases their replacement by office entrances, made Bath Street a relatively deserted and depressing place. That was not helped by the fact that the Cross Bath terminating the view looking west, had been unsympathetically altered on several occasions and had become dirty and dismal. The situation has now been transformed: the Cross Bath has been restored, the Hot Bath is now a medical treatment centre, and Nick Grimshaw's beautiful new spa building is intended to act as the necessary magnet to draw people into Bath Street. The New Private Baths were demolished in 1889 and rebuilt with an additional storey by the City Architect, Major Charles E. Davis, who, however gallant an officer he may have been, was less than dashing here. He did preserve Baldwin's colonnade however, which was again preserved when his dull building was demolished in about 1970 and replaced by a single-storey structure.

Baldwin's sequence of streets and spaces around the Baths were a new phenomenon in Bath, and to some extent in the country as a whole. All the streets described in previous chapters of this book were on virgin sites, but Bath Street, Union Street, and the improved Stall Street were carved out of an existing urban fabric. They had to create a sequence just as satisfying as Wood's from Queen Square to the Royal Crescent, but unlike his they had to adjust it to existing features and incorporate some of them into it, and do it in such a way that they looked as natural a part of it as the new buildings. Baldwin faced problems that John Wood did not: he needed all Wood's skills, but he had to develop new ones. He also needed administrative skills that Wood did not. From this period onwards urban planners not only needed aesthetic design skills, they had to be valuers and able to negotiate with property owners. Increasingly they had to know how the parliamentary system worked, be able to influence the framing of Bills, and become adept at giving evidence to Parliamentary Committees. More and more they had to become administrators. Eventually this would lead to the disastrous modern situation where town planners are scarcely ever designers in any sense that Wood and Baldwin were. Above all, Baldwin was an urban planner of a type quite different to Wood, having to base his plans on the constraints imposed by existing buildings and streets, without the luxury of developing on open fields.

5　My account of this tragic episode, but not my conclusion, is based on Jane Root's admirable researches published in vol.5 of *Bath History*, 1994.

Unfortunately there was one administrative skill he did not have. In October 1791 the Corporation asked to see his books.[5] He prevaricated. Nine months later, after several further

requests had been ignored, they discharged him from all his duties and decided to take proceedings against him. He was warned of this in a friendly note but ignored it. After a delay of six months the Council filed a Bill in Chancery alleging that he had carried out his duties with carelessness amounting to negligence and had been guilty of false accounting. After a subpoena had been issued against him, Baldwin replied that he couldn't answer it without access to documents in the Council's possession, which were apparently then given to him. Events were overtaken in September 1793 when Baldwin was declared bankrupt, along with most builders and craftsmen in Bath, as well as several of the city's banks. His possessions were sold and in the following September auditors appointed by his debtors declared that he owed the Corporation £2,824, and again asked for his books. He never supplied them.

Previous writers have assumed that Baldwin had been dishonest. That is indeed possible, but there is an alternative and to me more probable explanation. He had taken on far more work than he could control – City Architect and Surveyor, Deputy Chamberlain, Inspector of the Baths, with all the onerous and petty day-to-day duties that involved, in addition to his great works in the centre of the city and at Bathwick. He was presumably incapable of effective delegation. It seems probable that while working on his speculative developments, for which he had to account to nobody, he had got into the disastrous habit of neglecting his book-keeping, or even of not keeping any systematic records at all, and the reason he never delivered his books to the Council is that they didn't exist, or if they did, in fragmentary and incomplete form, probably with piles of invoices and receipts stuffed into drawers. Under such intolerable pressure he was becoming stretched to breaking point and probably close to breakdown. Like plenty of people before and since, he tried to put his worries out of his mind by working on something more satisfying. Instead of working day and night to pull his accounts together he spent his hours preparing a book of his designs. It never appeared, no doubt because his bankruptcy killed it. Baldwin was undoubtedly guilty of administrative incompetence, but the weight of evidence suggests that he was not dishonest. No forged receipts or documents were ever produced, he was never charged in a court of law, and he was discharged from bankruptcy in 1802 without protests from anybody. The case against him was based on an assumption, that his failure to produce the account books was evidence of fraud, but there was no positive evidence whatever.

At his discharge from bankruptcy Baldwin was 52. He lived for another eighteen years and built nothing further in Bath, but had some success elsewhere. His most notable subsequent works were the extremely fascinating rebuilding of Hafod House in Cardiganshire which no longer survives, and the lovely Town Hall at Devizes, which fortunately does. His legacy to Bath was immense – two superb buildings in Milsom Street, the Guildhall, the Cross Bath, the east side of Stall Street, Bath Street, Laura Place and Great Pulteney Street, to list only his finest achievements.

8 From Attica to Tuscany

In the eighteenth century there was only one instance of an architect of national reputation being brought into Bath to design a building – Robert Adam. In the nineteenth century that practice became more common, and started with a rush just after 1800 when the Greek Revival became suddenly fashionable, and a few property owners in Bath wanted an architect who had built a Greek building, which no Bath architect had done.

It is curious that since the revival of classical architecture in fifteenth-century Italy, architects who had studied the ruins of ancient Roman buildings with such devotion had taken no interest whatever in the remains of ancient Greek buildings, although they knew from Vitruvius and other Roman authors that classical architecture, and its Doric, Ionic and Corinthian orders, arose in Greece. Although in the eighteenth century Ottoman Greece was not very safe for travellers, a considerable number of people had visited Athens and brought back information about the surviving remains, and as early as 1682 the French Jacob Spon and the English George Wheler had published their *Voyage d'Italie, de Dalmatie, de Grèce et du Levant* which described the Acropolis and included a not very revealing engraving of it, including the Parthenon. This lack of interest is even more curious since there were easily accessible Greek temples in southern Italy which were not studied until drawings of those at Paestum were published in France in 1764. The so-called Temple of Neptune there is the best preserved of all Greek temples.

Before then, as a result of encouragement and help from the aristocratic Society of Dilettanti, two architects, James Stuart and Nicholas Revett, had spent two years in Athens drawing and measuring the remains. On their return they published the first volume of their *Antiquities of Athens* in 1762, which contained engravings of relatively minor buildings, and in 1789 a second volume dealing with the great Periclean buildings on the Acropolis. Two further volumes appeared later. In 1759 Stuart had designed the first Greek building in Britain, a Doric temple in the grounds of Hagley in Worcestershire. At the same time, in Paris Soufflot used Greek Doric columns in the crypt of what is now the Pantheon. Despite notorious laziness, Stuart was responsible for several other Greek buildings and became known as Athenian Stuart. A few other architects followed, but the Greek Revival, a late phase of European Neo-Classicism, didn't take off until after 1800.

One of the architects who followed Stuart's lead was J. M. Gandy (1771-1843), a superb draughtsman who had won the Gold Medal at the Royal Academy Schools in 1790 and worked for a while in the office of John Soane, who supported his election as an Associate Academician in

111 Doric House, south
front. J. M. Gandy, 1805

1803 and gave him and his family financial help throughout his life. Gandy was responsible for few buildings, and is best known today for the many superb watercolour perspectives he drew over the years for Soane. In 1803 he exhibited at the RA a first design for Doric House at the top of Cavendish Road in Bath, to be the home and exhibition gallery of the painter Thomas Barker, describing it as being then under construction. The modified design which was actually built was the first unmistakeably Greek building in the city. Doric House's pedimented south-facing front is conventional and charming, with a small central window on the first floor and a larger one below it. (111) The long east-facing street elevation is neither conventional nor charming. It is in fact somewhat ungainly, but extremely fascinating and original: there is no other building like it, anywhere. (112) The steep fall in the site is utilised to accommodate the domestic offices in a stylobate on which the rest of the house sits. The wall above is set well back from the front of the stylobate so that a row of detached unfluted Doric columns can sit on it, with antae (matching pilasters) at each end. At this level the wall has no windows because this was Barker's exhibition gallery for which he needed plenty of blank wall. The columns support a full Doric entablature on top of which is a row of smaller Doric columns in antis and their entablature. The larger Greek Doric temples had two storeys of columns internally to support their roofs, but two storeys were never used externally as here. Very few Greek examples of this survive, but one of those that do is the Temple of 'Neptune' at Paestum, which Gandy would have known because Soane had just bought the drawings upon which Thomas Major based his *Ruins of Paestum*, and Gandy had constant access to Soane's library and collections.

112 Doric House, street elevation

Each of Gandy's columns has a concave echinus in its capital, instead of the more powerful convex cushion moulding of all actual Greek Doric columns. The roof is adorned with antefixes over the columns.

While Gandy was building Doric House, a more distinguished architect was invited to Bath, George Dance junior (1741-1825). He knew Bath well and had already shown his admiration of John Wood's urban planning by creating London's first circus and crescent. He also knew John Palmer well, not the architect, but the wealthy brewer, MP, mayor of Bath and proprietor of the Theatres Royal in Bath and Bristol. (The two men's identical names have caused much confusion to some of Bath's historians.) By 1804 the old Bath theatre in Orchard Street was too small and becoming dilapidated, so Palmer commissioned Dance to design a new one on the present site in the Sawclose. Today only the original entrance front on Beauford Square survives because in 1862 the theatre was gutted in a fire and rebuilt

113 Theatre Royal. Original entrance front on Beauford Square. George Dance junior, 1805

by C. J. Phipps, who gave it the horrible new entrance on Sawclose which partially obscures the Georgian house in which Beau Nash lived. The result is that Dance's front has now become the side, hidden away from theatre-goers in Beauford Square. (113) Its design consists of a three-storey windowed block set forward from plain-walled wings, and with a long row of windows set in arches running at ground level across the façade. The upper two floors have giant deeply panelled pilasters with caps consisting of Greek masks, with swags between them. The roof has Greek lyres over the four outer pilasters, and a large royal coat of arms with its lion and unicorn supporters over the central two. Originally the main entrance was in the centre with entrances on each side for the pit and galleries. This lovely façade's most prominent and attractive features are the panelled pilasters, a form very rarely used in Britain, but more frequently met in Italy, where Dance would have seen them during his youthful six years there, perhaps the very similar ones in the Cappella Paolina in Santa Maria Maggiore in Rome. By the 1970s Dance's façade had become extremely dilapidated, but it was given an exemplary restoration in 1982 and the theatre's range of productions widened by the building of the fly tower which rises up behind the façade. Despite the façade's decorative features and wonderfully lively skyline, it is quiet and restrained, obviously far too much so for Victorian taste in the 1860s when the theatre was partially rebuilt. One of Dance's achievements here is the way he related it to the 1730s terraces facing and flanking it, thus making it the only public building in Bath to have created a formal urban space. This contribution to Bath's urban planning is far too seldom recognised, and at the moment is not treated in a way to make anything of it. The little fenced lawn is pathetic.

We must now pass from the sparklingly Thespian to the dismally Sabbatarian – to the Walcot Methodist Chapel. (114) It was built in 1815-16 by the Rev. William Jenkins (c.1763-1844), who had trained as an architect before becoming a Wesleyan minister. After 20 years as an itinerant preacher he returned to his original calling and set up in London as an architect of Methodist chapels. In this specialised field he developed a substantial reputation, building at least 16 chapels throughout the country. No doubt his long years preaching had made him highly expert in meeting the functional needs of the chapels he designed, but he had little skill in making them attractive externally – but then the architectural glory of Dissenting chapels is usually their interiors, rarely their exteriors. The Walcot Chapel's Greek Doric porch with columns correctly without bases, displays Williams' architectural knowledge (or the contents of his library) but the composition of arched windows and Corinthian pilasters is unhappy, as are the gable and pediment above, which is only minimally related to everything else.

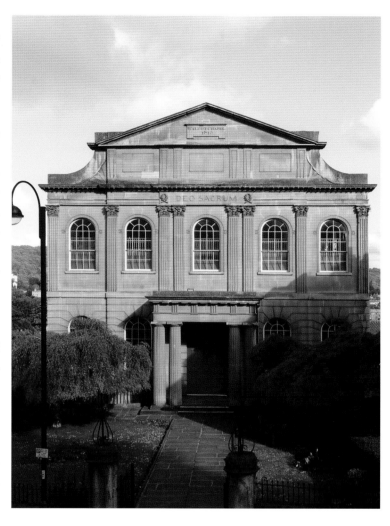

114 Walcot Methodist Chapel. Rev. William Jenkins, 1816

The next London architect to work in Bath, William Wilkins (1778-1839), was much more distinguished and soon to become more so when he designed London's University College in Gower Street and the National Gallery in Trafalgar Square. The son of an architect, he was educated at Caius College, Cambridge, which gave him a travelling scholarship to spend four years in Italy and Greece, and then elected him a Fellow. His first major work was Downing College in Cambridge. In 1809, whilst that was under construction, he was commissioned to add a Greek Doric portico to the Lower Assembly Rooms in Bath (demolished in 1933). It apparently impressed local opinion because in 1817 the Freemasons employed him to build their Hall in York Street. (It is now the Friends' Meeting House.) (115) The front is masterly. Set on a low stylobate is a portico with Greek Ionic columns in antis, projecting from what were originally plain side wings, but each of which now contain a window. The doorway inside the portico is blind, and said to have always been so, which if true makes the portico a nonsense, a magnificent clipped-on bit of Greek dressing. The two actual entrances are set back on either

side in very un-Greek arches in rusticated walls. Internally the Great Room is lit only by a pair of lanterns in the roof, neatly solving the problem of putting windows in a Greek temple, which real Greek temples never had.

Opposite the Freemasons' Hall is a terrace of five houses which also have Greek details. (116) Their architect is unknown. Several writers have argued that the coincidence of two Greek buildings being in such close proximity in Palladian Bath suggests that they were designed by the same architect. I think it is unlikely. The Freemasons' Hall is powerfully three-dimensional and the façade opposite is not, it is very notably flat. Its poorly designed pilasters project minimally from the wall, the projection of the centrepiece is so slight that it is scarcely perceptible, and since its pilasters are identical to all the others it makes so little impact that it is superfluous. The terrace would look scarcely different without it. I cannot believe that Wilkins designed this ineffectual façade.

Partis College on Newbridge Hill, an almshouse for 'decayed gentlewomen', was built and endowed under the will of the Rev. Fletcher Partis. (117) It is one of Bath's most surprising and impressive building layouts, clearly based closely on William Wilkins's Downing College in Cambridge. It was built in 1825-7 by two architects of such obscurity that only one other building by them is known, a cheap and unappealing Gothic church in Mill Hill. They were Samuel Flood Page (1796-1854) and his brother Philip (1798-?), sons of an almost equally obscure

116 Terrace in York Street. Possibly by William Wilkins, c.1820

London builder and architect. The only other known fact about them is that Samuel later gave up architecture and was ordained into the Church of England.

It was quite usual for almshouses to be organised on a collegiate pattern as this one is, with the individual houses grouped in a quadrangle and focussing on a chapel which, with its chaplain, was the centre of the community's corporate life. Each house has its own front door and four rooms on two floors. The chapel dominates the great quad, being the tallest building in the complex, its windowless attic rising behind the portico. The Ionic columns are based, like those at Downing College, on the Erectheion in Athens (known to architects through Stuart and Revett's *Antiquities of Athens*). The layout consists of three ranges. The south-facing middle one is organised conventionally with three pavilions, the central of which is the chapel. Its slightly projecting end pavilions are articulated by single Doric pilasters between the windows, doubled at each end. Their plain parapet rises slightly higher than the one on the adjoining houses, and rises higher still over the central window. The east and west ranges are half as long as the central one and therefore need only end pavilions, which are identical to those in the central range. In 1863 George Gilbert Scott magnificently Gothicised the interior of the chapel. Partis College, hidden from sight at Newbridge Hill, immaculately maintained, externally unaltered, and in sparkling condition, is one of Bath's least known treasures: William Wilkins's gift to the city by Flood Page proxy.

After the completion of Partis College, the influx of London architects ceased for a while. In 1820 John Pinch was commissioned by the Duke of Cleveland, who had inherited the Bathwick estate after the death of Henrietta Laura Pulteney, and controlled the Kennet and Avon Canal Company, to design the company's headquarters office by building it on a bridge over the canal where it passes under Sydney Road. (118) The result is a very handsome building, but a remarkably old-fashioned one, still Palladian and without a trace of Greek influence. The arched ground-floor windows have Pinch's usual white-painted frames recessed into arches, and the rectangular windows on the first floor have the usual flat entablatures flanking a pedimented central one. Internally the lofty board-room survives, and at the back there is space for the tow-horses to manoeuvre as the path changes to the opposite side of the canal. It is said that there was a hatch in the floor so that packages could be dropped into the barges as they rushed through.

A change which occurred in the years around 1800 was mentioned in Chapter 1 – the developing Romantic appreciation of wild nature and the desire of householders to be in the closest contact with their gardens and the landscape beyond. In the decades after 1800 the sunny side of terrace houses were increasingly being designed with balconies on which the occupants could sit in the open air, almost as if they were on the terrace of a country house. Many had tent-like metal roofs. Access was either through French doors or, when the sash windows were large enough, through them. They became so popular that many owners of older houses wanted them, so they had balconies fixed onto their façades and lowered their window

118 The Kennet and Avon Canal, bridged by the elder John Pinch's 1820 Cleveland House and the splendid road bridge by the canal's engineer John Rennie, c.1805

cills to near floor level so that they could step onto them. A compromise used on some houses, particularly when the orientation of a terrace meant that drawing-room windows did not face the sun, was to fix a balconette for potted plants on those which did. In previous centuries balconies and their balusters were constructed of stone, which gave an effect of heaviness which was usually unwelcome in the Regency, when lightness and elegance were required. These qualities were perfectly met by iron balconies, which had the additional advantage of being transparent, thus giving minimal obstruction to sunlight. Way back in the 1770s the Adam brothers were amongst the first architects to use them. At that date they and a few other architects had to design them themselves and have them made up, but by the 1820s demand

119 By far the most popular pattern for Regency balcony rails consisted of slim crossed rods, half-jointed and secured by cast lead or iron stars. Darlington Street

120 Cast-iron balcony in Vane Street

121 By 1830 taste had begun to prefer the heavier forms which resulted from iron casting. At that period Greek decorative motifs, such as the anthemia in this Cleveland Place balconette, were almost invariably used

was so great that iron founders and smiths produced them industrially and sold them through catalogues. At this period it was inevitable that Greek decorative forms, such as anthemia, running scrolls, and so on, should be popular, but one of the most frequently used and most beautiful patterns was a simple network of slim rods half-jointed where they crossed, and the crossings secured by iron or lead stars. (119)

At the bottom of Bathwick Hill is Raby Place, a four-storey terrace of 1818-25, designed, as its ramped cornices proclaim, by John Pinch. Most of the houses have tented balconies. (75) After that date in Bath, but not in other cities, although the building of terraces continued, they catered for the growing working population and were no longer for comfortably-off people. They wanted villas. Some villas had less accommodation than the houses in most of the terraces, but they had fewer stairs, bigger gardens, and by that date enjoyed a higher social prestige. The most interesting were built on Bathwick Hill to take advantage of the spectacular views looking south. An early example is Spa Villa, an enchanting house of 1820 by Pinch. (122) It was originally an irregular octagon, but in 1877 the canted garden side was altered and its simple geometry spoilt. As seen from the road however, the house remains as Pinch designed it, with its wide overhanging roof, and a window cut simply into each of the three visible canted faces. The Villa is approached from the road through a delightful archway set in the boundary wall, which curves up on either side to support it. Its design was a sign of things to come. It consists of two simple rectangular piers topped by un-moulded rectangular blocks of stone acting as a cornice from which the arch springs. As we shall see, in a few years time another young Bath architect would design some small structures consisting almost entirely of un-moulded rectangular blocks of stone.

In addition to his classical buildings, Pinch designed several churches in Bath and elsewhere, which, being Gothic, will not be discussed here. He had a son, also called John (? – 1849) who continued his practice. Almost all the son's recorded work, both ecclesiastical and domestic, was Gothic, but he built one important classical building in Bath which is quite impressive but enormously infuriating. It is the central block on the west side of Queen Square mentioned in Chapter 4. (123) As explained there, Wood had intended that side of the Square to be similar to the one opposite, but a recalcitrant leaseholder insisted that his mansion should be set back behind a forecourt in the centre of the side. Wood dealt with that by building very beautiful Palladian blocks of three houses on either side of the forecourt. Because of the slope they are built at different levels, but being separated by the gap this was of no consequence. The result was a resounding success. This happy state of affairs lasted for the better part of a century until 1830, when the younger Pinch was commissioned to fill the gap with a block of three houses. By then early Georgian buildings seemed hopelessly dull and old-fashioned, so he would have felt little compulsion to make his work fit harmoniously with Wood's, though he had the taste not to use his favourite Gothic. His block is a fascinating design when looked at on its own, but makes a dreadful neighbour. Wood's blocks have three moderately high storeys, his has three much

122 Spa Villa. John Pinch the elder, c.1820. 1980s photograph before the trees obscured the view

taller ones, as well as an attic storey over the central house and a tall balustrade over its other two. Wood's façades are very simple, with large areas of blank wall; Pinch's is crammed with incident, fluted Greek Doric half columns in the centre and unfluted pilasters at the sides. Wood's cornices are small, Pinch has a very deep heavily modelled entablature and cornice which draws attention to the discrepancy in level of Wood's two pavilions. Each of Wood's pediments has three vases, Pinch has a Greek termination on top of his ten pilasters and columns. Wood's two blocks are characteristically early-eighteenth-century Palladian, Pinch's anticipate Victorian richness and splendour. This clash of cultures is unpleasant. On its own, or in more suitable company, Pinch's building would be splendid, but here it looks like showing-off, a deliberate attempt to demonstrate the superiority of the 1830s to the 1730s, and of course, of Pinch to Wood.

In the eighteenth and nineteenth centuries Bath produced a series of fine architects, most of them the sons of Bath builders. The greatest was unquestionably the elder Wood, but two others were notably brilliant – Thomas Baldwin whose work was discussed in the previous two chapters, and Henry Edmund Goodridge (1797-1864). Goodridge's father, a successful builder who was responsible for much of the later work at Bathwick, articled his son to John Lowder, a minor Bath architect. In his early twenties the young Goodridge set up in independent practice in Bath and rapidly demonstrated outstanding skills. His first relatively major work was Argyle Chapel of 1821, of which the façade was most unfortunately altered in 1861. It consisted of an Ionic portico at ground level and an attic above. The attic had very curious stumpy Doric pilasters, which were a more extreme version of Soane's pilasters in the attic storey of his Bank of England's Threadneedle Street façade. Here, right at the beginning of his

123 The central block in the west side of Queen Square. John Pinch junior, 1830

career, Goodridge was demonstrating his fondness for making his own variations of long-established classical elements.

Then, while still in his mid-twenties, he had the good fortune of being chosen as architect by the enormously wealthy William Beckford, a bisexual with a pronounced weakness for young men. Beckford was famous for having built the towering Fonthill Abbey which he had recently sold (fortunately for him, because it collapsed a few years later). For his new home he had bought the end houses in Lansdown Crescent and Lansdown Place West which were separated from each other by the lane leading to the mews at the back. He commissioned Goodridge to link them by a bridge. (124) It is a delightfully modest design, with none of Pinch's shouting down of its older neighbours. In fact it

124 Lansdown Crescent. The bridge connecting the two houses owned by William Beckford. H.E. Goodridge

is an early example of keeping in keeping, consisting of a shallow segmental arch, three simple windows, and a balustraded parapet like the one on the adjoining houses. Beckford then bought land at the back which extended to the top of Lansdown Hill, and after obtaining designs from several London and Bath architects, commissioned Goodridge to build a lookout tower on the summit, which was completed in 1824. (125)

Whether sexual attraction was a factor in Beckford's appointment of Goodridge is unknowable, but historians have assumed that the reason for choosing a young architect was that he would be more malleable than an older and more experienced one. It probably was a factor: the millionaire Beckford was strong-minded and used to getting his own way. He was knowledgeable about architecture and a passionate collector of paintings and objects of virtú. He had a justifiable belief in his own artistic taste. There can be little doubt that much of the Tower's design was strongly influenced by him, but there can be no doubt whatever that the details of the design were Goodridge's, and God is in the details.

By the 1820s most architects had to be willing and able to work in classical or medieval styles, and most of them, like Goodridge, clearly enjoyed doing both. He even liked to mix them together. His first designs for the Tower were medieval in style. The final, built, design consisted of two major elements, a tall tower rising out of a picturesque Italianate cluster of different one and two-storey blocks. The single-storey block contained the kitchen, its offices and a bedroom, the two-storey block fronted by an entrance loggia contained the rooms in which Beckford displayed his treasures. An apsidal chapel made a third block at the rear. On the east side there is a pair of high chimney stacks united by an arch with a heavy cornice. The tower rises sheer and without ornament for about a hundred feet, up to a large entablature and cornice, which have the effect of giving the tower something of the proportions of a classical

125 Beckford's Tower.
H.E. Goodridge, 1824

column. Above this is the look-out belvedere, a room with three arched plate-glass windows on each side, deeply recessed into rectangular openings. (126) The belvedere has its own entablature and cornice, above which is a panel of Greek key and another cornice. The contrast between the deeply shadowed windows and the extreme delicacy of the entablature is enchanting. The next stage is octagonal, its cast-iron balusters supporting iron vases. Set back behind the parapet rises the superb lantern, an octagonal paraphrase of the circular Choragic monument of Lysicrates, though nothing is copied from it, every detail is invented. The heavily fluted iron columns for example have capitals which are a sort of Grecianised Egyptian, and the entablature is so complex as to be beyond brief analysis. In the tiled roof the junctions of four of the eight slopes are covered by iron scrolls. The roof is crowned by an elaborate finial as in the Choragic monument, but quite different in detail. The lantern was gilded, and at dusk as it caught the last rays of the sun could be seen from miles away, as it now can again, the gilding having been spectacularly renewed.

Beckford wanted to be buried in his garden at the foot of the Tower, but its being unconsecrated land that was not possible, so he was buried in the Abbey Cemetery and the Tower and garden were sold. When his daughter, the Duchess of Hamilton, heard that they were going to be turned into a beer garden she bought them back and in 1848 gave them to the parish for use as a cemetery. She then commissioned Goodridge to build its railings and gateway. The latter is a curious mixture of Norman details and Italianate form, with a profusion of mottos and symbols of death and resurrection. Beckford's remains and the huge granite sarcophagus which he had designed himself, were then moved into the new cemetery.

126 Beckford's Tower. The look-out belvedere and lantern

The tower is superlative, one of Bath's most beautiful buildings, much smaller but far more inventive than James Wyatt's enormous heap of Gothic details at Fonthill. The young Goodridge was not perfect however. The relationship between the tower and the house out of which it grows is poor, especially when seen from the road. It is clear that Goodridge was aware of this, because 25 years later he drew a new design for the house, raising it in height and making it an assemblage of verticals. It is probably fortunate that it wasn't built because, although the relationship would have been better, the lower part of the tower would have been obscured, and its column-like proportion lost.

It seems probable that Goodridge's next building in Bath was the Bazaar in Quiet Street, which was attributed to him by Walter Ison in 1948, but for which no confirmation has yet been found. (127) The attribution seems reasonable because at that time, 1824-5, there was no other architect in Bath with the inventiveness and sensitivity to have been responsible. The first floor, which survives more or less intact, is a large hall which was used for auctions, lectures, exhibitions etc. Its ceiling consists of three shallow saucer domes separated from each other by segmental arches. Daylight comes from a glass lantern in each dome and large windows at each end of the room. The façade consists of one of these large Adamish tripartite windows under a segmental arch and iron fanlight, set between wide piers with niches containing Grecian statues of Genius and Commerce

127 The Bazaar, Quiet Street. Probably by H. E. Goodridge, 1824-5

carved by the Bath sculptor, Lucius Gahagan. The parapet is divided into three parts reflecting the divisions below, the central one stepped back to support a third statue. Walter Ison recognised that the parapet is based closely on the Choragic Monument of Thrassylus illustrated in Stuart and Revett's *Antiquities of Athens*. The Greek original had a row of circular wreaths in its frieze. That was not possible in the Bazaar because the arch would have made them look cramped. Instead there is a single wreath centred over each niche. With the elegance

128 Cleveland Bridge.
H.E. Goodridge, 1827.
The steel trusses
below the roadway
are modern

of its parts and their impeccably judged proportions, this surviving part of the façade is extremely lovely.

By 1825 Goodridge had enough capital to be able to make a substantial building speculation of his own, no doubt with a large mortgage. This was the shopping arcade called The Corridor running from the High Street to Union Street, an early example of a building type which was to remain popular throughout the nineteenth century. Unfortunately Goodridge's timber and coloured glass roof was demolished in 1870 and replaced by the present barrel-vaulted iron and glass roof, and all the shopfronts were replaced. Only the entrance façade on the High Street survives. It is five bays wide, with the central three slightly recessed, an attic with three lunette windows, and in the centre above it a length of wall decorated with a wreath and festoon. This top part of the façade shows the influence of Soane's now destroyed block in Oxford Street. Soane, as we shall see, was becoming a major influence on Bath's architects, as he was almost everywhere at this time.

Goodridge was the Surveyor to the Bathwick estate, which in 1827 commissioned him to design a new bridge over the Avon to replace a ferry. (128) At first inevitably known as the New Bridge, it later got its present name, Cleveland Bridge, after the Duke of Cleveland who had inherited

129 Cleveland Bridge.
One of the four toll
houses

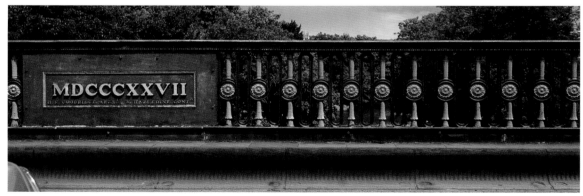

130 Cleveland Bridge.
The cast-iron balustrade

the estate. Like the top of the Lansdown Tower it is a fascinating mixture of the latest iron technology with the most ancient Greek aesthetic. The cast-iron ribs, which span a little over 100 feet, spring from masonry abutments which support four little toll-houses with one storey at road level and two below it. They each have squat but curiously attractive porticos facing the roadway, with four widely spaced primitive Doric columns, correctly without bases, and somewhat less usually, without triglyths and metopes. (129) The bottom third of the columns are unfluted, a feature occasionally used in Greek buildings, no doubt for the same reason it was used here, as protection against damage from the wheels of carriages and carts. The porticos were not entrances, as they were in Greek temples, but gave shelter to the people paying tolls at the guichets which took the place of doors. The design of the bridge's heavy cast-iron balustrades is highly imaginative and original in its clever but sparing use of Greek decorative details. (130) The centres of both balustrades have cast-iron panels giving the date 1827 and the name of the architect. Clearly Goodridge was on good terms with his client to have been allowed to do this so prominently.

While the bridge was under construction Goodridge built the triangular Cleveland Place as the approach to it. Here the influence of Soane is very clear, for example at 9 Cleveland Place West, which has Soane's typical incised decoration on either side of the slightly recessed centre. (131) (It is possible that the incisions are now rather more prominent than Goodridge expected, because they have retained the soot which has washed off everything else.) The central element of the tripartite window on the first floor is an example of Goodridge's use of an invented feature instead of the expected conventional one: instead of a pediment he has designed an equivalently triangular composition consisting of a circular wreath and two festoons. There is a delightful collection of cast- and wrought-iron balconies throughout the Place.

131 9 Cleveland Place, c.1830. H.E. Goodridge showing the influence of John Soane

Years later, in 1848 when he was 51, Goodridge designed another building in Cleveland Place, the beautiful Dispensary on its east side. (132) It was built for a charity set up in 1832 to give medical care to impoverished sick people in Bath and the surrounding district. It would appear that Goodridge had become more conservative in his middle age because in many ways the design is a return to Palladianism, although the finesse of the mouldings, the emphasised pediments over the windows, and the crammed frontispiece contrasting with the plain walls on each side, are clues to its later date.

Even clearer examples of Soane's influence are four pairs of small semi-detached houses in Claremont Place, which were built in 1817 by an unknown architect. (133) As mentioned earlier, in the decades around 1800 people of sensibility wanted their houses to be in the closest contact with nature. The detached house set in its own grounds was the ideal, the terrace house had become the least desirable, and the semi became, and has remained right up to our own day, the acceptable English compromise between the two (semis are rare in other countries). In the Claremont Place houses the end pilasters with their incised ornament and terminal acroteria are typically Soanian, and the segmental-headed windows set in segmental-headed

132 Dispensary in
Cleveland Place.
H.E.Goodridge, 1848

recesses equally so. The way the architect used blank windows to deal with the problem of providing a central feature to hold the design together when the party wall made real windows impossible, was not very clever but became the most frequently used solution to the problem.

There are many other examples of Soane's influence in Bath. A tiny but very attractive one is a porch added in about 1830 to an earlier house at 24 Great Stanhope Street. (134) It was

133 Soanian semi-detached
houses in Claremont
Place, 1817

134 Soanian porch at 24
Great Stanhope Street.
Edward Davis c.1830

designed by, and introduces us to, Edward Davis (1802-52), a most interesting architect who had been a pupil of Soane. Born in Bath, he was the son of Charles Davis, a prosperous minor painter, and appears to have been comfortably off throughout his life. At the end of his two years with Soane, in 1826 he started his own practice in Bath. After a few minor works, including some Gothic houses in Entry Hill and a Soanian toll-house at Bailbrook, he established himself firmly when in 1829 a committee of local worthies selected him to design the 46-acre Royal Victoria Park, which they, with encouragement from the Corporation, were then promoting. It was opened in 1830 by the Duchess of Kent and her young daughter the future Queen Victoria, and survives very little altered today. It was an early precursor of the hundreds of public parks which were opened during her reign, many of them to provide green spaces in congested and airless towns, though Bath certainly didn't come into that category.

The Park is delightful, with the belts of trees, serpentine lake and winding paths usual in gentlemen's parks at that time, all of them strongly influenced by John Loudon's prolific writings. The Park has its inevitable *cottage ornée* for the park-keeper, and gates at the entrances enabling the

135 Royal Victoria Park gateway. Edward Davis, 1830

park to be locked at night. (The iron gates were taken for munitions during the war.) At the Marlborough Lane entrance the carriageway is flanked by stone pedestrian gateways. (135) Each is simply an assembly of large vertical blocks of stone supporting a tiny arched attic, taking to a logical conclusion the simplicity of Spa Villa's little gateway on Bathwick Hill. It is classical architecture reduced to the minimum, to how it could be imagined to have started in its infancy. Michael Forsyth has suggested, probably correctly, that Davis took the germ of his idea from St John's Church at Bethnal Green on which he was working during his last few months in Soane's office, but the clusters of un-moulded brick piers in the Mausoleum at Dulwich are a closer parallel. Whichever, Davis took the idea further than Soane ever did.

Soane was influenced by the French Jesuit architectural theorist Abbé Laugier, and possibly introduced Davis to his books, most notably the hugely influential *Essai sur l'architecture* of 1753. It proposed that classical architecture was a development from the primitive hut mentioned by Vitruvius, and it turned architects towards a liking for primitive forms. A notable follower was Ledoux, as demonstrated for example by his salt works at Arc et Senans. Soane, long before Davis became his pupil, had prepared an unpublished translation of Laugier's *Observations sur l'architecture*. Davis's beautiful primitive gate piers are a late, but historically important, result of Laugier's theories.

In 1837 the Park was given a splendid new ornament, an obelisk to mark Princess Victoria's eighteenth birthday. (136) It was designed by the City Architect G. P. Manners (c.1789-1866). An extremely beautiful design, it is also a very clever one because Manners found a way to make his version different from any of the countless other obelisks in Europe. Unlike the Egyptian prototypes which are square in section, his is triangular in cross section, and rises out of a triangular base which curves down to three recumbent lions. There is a delightful profile portrait of the Princess carved on the base. The obelisk is surrounded by a balustrade. Before it was finished Victoria had become Queen.

In 1840 the 24-year-old architect James Wilson (1816-1900) was offered the commission of designing Walcot Schools to accommodate up to 1000 pupils in a single building on a small irregularly shaped site on the precipitous slope of Guinea Lane, which tumbles down from Lansdown Hill to the London Road. A more established architect would probably have said that the site was impossible and the budget too small, but Wilson accepted the challenge. As so often happens, these daunting restrictions brought out the best in him: the Schools are a triumph. In what turned out to be a very long career he proved to be a most interesting designer, though as most of his work was either Gothic or occasionally Norman it is outside the scope of this book. However, with William Wilcox with whom he was in partnership from 1867, he was responsible for the classical Grand Pump Room Hotel which is described in the next chapter.[1] He had emerged three years before building the Walcot Schools when, at the absurdly youthful age of 21, he was selected to design the huge Queen's College on Claverton Down, which was intended to be the basis of a new university. Alas for young Wilson, the

1 His best known buildings are the Kingswood and Royal High Schools of 1852 and 1856 respectively. His best churches are the Gothic St Stephen's (1845) at the top of Lansdown Road, the fascinating St Paul's (now Holy Trinity) in Monmouth Street (1873), and the classical Moravian Chapel described in the next chapter.

136 Obelisk in Royal
Victoria Park.
G.P. Manners, 1837

building never got beyond the foundations. Perhaps he was given the Walcot Schools commission as a recompense.

The Schools have recently been converted into flats and the stonework cleaned. The building's most interesting face is the cliff-like façade on Guinea Lane, two storeys high at the upper end and four at the bottom, the two lower ones being treated as a basement (crammed with classrooms). (137) The basement windows are topped by a deep but plain entablature and cornice. The upper two rows of windows are set within a very plain arcade, the arches supported by wide flat pilasters which declare very clearly that they are the main load-bearing elements. The two qualities which are immediately noticeable are the plainness of the façade and the great depth of the window reveals, conveying an impression of great solidity and weight. It is surprising that, as far as I am aware, no previous writers have described this superb building.

Indeed, it appears to have made very little splash when it was built. The reason, of course, is that the budget ensured that its plainness and relative lack of ornament, at a time when Ruskin was shortly to write that ornament 'is the chief part of architecture' made it of very little interest to people in the 1840s. But Ruskin also wrote that 'No person who is not a great sculptor or painter *can* be an architect. If he is not a sculptor or painter, he can only be a builder'. It is the sculptural quality of these great slabs of stone (138) which make this little building so great. The arches and the few bits of ornament are superfluous, though they were essential in 1840.

139 Montebello, Bathwick Hill. H.E. Goodridge, 1828. 1980s photograph

In the early nineteenth century, when Europe was obsessed with the Picturesque, Bath was considered to be sadly lacking in its qualities. Uvedale Price, the theorist of the Picturesque, remembered 'my disappointment the first time I approached Bath....how little the buildings are made to yield to the ground, and how few trees are mixed with them'. By not yielding to the ground he was referring to the way that the great terraces and crescents are imposed upon the undulating terrain, and didn't respond, in his opinion, closely enough to it by stepping up and down or back and forward. Eighteenth-century Bath is the archetypical example of classical geometrical buildings imposed upon a rolling hillside, just as Italian hill towns are the archetypical examples of romantically organic houses rolling over the hillside. Classical architects, such as John Wood and Le Corbusier, exulted in their mastery of the terrain, Romantic architects, such as John Nash and Frank Lloyd Wright, gloried in their adaptation to it.

Goodridge's tower on top of Lansdown Hill is gloriously Picturesque, so it isn't surprising that he built a Picturesque house for himself on Bathwick Hill. Two years after making his name with Beckford's tower, and three years after completing The Corridor, his speculative shopping arcade, the 31-year-old Goodridge had the financial resources to be able to do so. In 1828 he built himself a substantial villa on the upper slopes of Bathwick Hill. (139) Approached from the 1848 gate lodge by a steeply sloping drive, the house is a wonderful assembly of units of varying sizes, shapes and heights, adapted with studied asymmetry to the rising ground. The octagonal tower at the south-east corner based on the Greek first century AD Tower of the Winds, is flanked by a two-storey arched loggia, and the campanile to the rear is based on those Goodridge had sketched in Italy. Numerous roofs and elaborated chimneys produce a highly varied roofscape. With enviable mastery Goodridge fused these disparate units into a wonderfully picturesque whole. Alas, the octagonal tower has lost its upper stage and the house has lost its conservatory. It has even lost its beautiful and accurate name Montebello, which some prosaic later owner changed to Bathwick Grange.

In about 1814 the landscape painter Benjamin Barker (known as the English Poussin and brother of Thomas Barker who commissioned Gandy to design his house on Cavendish Road) had built the first house on the upper slopes of Bathwick Hill opposite the site later to be occupied by Montebello. It was square in plan and not Picturesque, its only notable feature being an arcade at ground level supporting a terrace looking over the very large garden. He probably designed the house himself and certainly designed the garden which was and remains intensely Picturesque. The site had the enormous benefit of containing a small spring which he designed to fall into a series of four stone-lined pools, the water cascading down from one to the other. The garden became famous and Queen Charlotte, a gardens enthusiast, came to see it.

In 1833 Barker decided to sell the house. It was bought by Edward Davis, who had laid out Victoria Park and had obviously fallen in love with Barker's 'hanging gardens, trout stream and woods' (as John Britton, the leading architectural writer of the time described them). Davis, who clearly had no financial problems, then remodelled the interior of the house and added a large wing, containing at the front a splendid dining room and the main bedroom with its own loggia. (140) At the back, stepping up the slope, were a picture gallery, kitchen, servants' quarters and coach house. Rising above was the by then almost inevitable Italianate look-out tower. The garden front has a large projecting bay containing a triple window on the ground floor which lights the dining room, and above it the tripartite loggia fronting Davis's bedroom. The low-pitched widely overhanging Italian roof breaks forward over the loggia, and from its

ridge emerges a wide chimney taking the place of the acroterion which a Greek temple would have. The result is that Barker's house has become a wing of a complex and Picturesque ensemble.

Internally much survives from Davis's time, including the beautiful and intact dining room. Its ceiling is slightly domed and has the starfish pattern that Soane used in his own dining room and elsewhere. The stair hall has further Soaneian details, one of them being the curious pelmet-like feature where the flat ceiling meets the sloping ceiling over the stair. Barker had called his house, which looks down to Smallcombe Valley, Smallcombe Villa. Davis renamed it Smallcombe Grove, and in 1856 it was changed to Oakwood, its present name.

Goodridge owned a considerable tract of land on the hillside, and in 1846-8 built three houses on it, Fiesole, a large detached villa for himself, and as a speculation, a pair of semi-detached houses which he called La Casetta and Casa Bianca. He then sold Montebello. The names tell us of the way his mind had developed. At that period English people were flocking to Tuscany

142 La Casetta (left) and
Casa Bianca. H.E.
Goodridge, 1846-8

where a fixed income went a great deal further than it did in England. Florence, with its wealth of Renaissance buildings, paintings and sculptures, was particularly favoured. Some of the English bought villas, and even palaces, which by comparison with English prices seemed extraordinarily cheap. Fiesole, the village which looks down to Florence and its noise, bustle and heat, soon housed a small English community. On Bathwick Hill Goodridge was building a miniature Fiesole to look down towards Bath.

His house, Fiesole, (141) is his usual Romantic cluster of Italianate blocks of various sizes and heights, wide overhanging shallow-pitched roofs and elaborate chimneys, but it also has a near replica of the tripartite bay and loggia projecting from a gable wall which Davis had added to his Smallcombe Grove 15 years earlier. This is a puzzle because few architects would wish to be seen imitating another architect's work quite so blatantly, and moreover, in such close proximity. One of the ways in which Goodridge's version differs from the original is that it has stone quoins and key-stones. I prefer to believe that it was his tribute to Davis for having wakened the Genius of the Place (an allegory which would have appealed to the English Poussin). Goodridge's pair of semi-detached villas (142) gave him a different opportunity to create an asymmetrical composition but with two gables, one for each house. There are the shallow-pitched widely overhanging roofs and the inevitable tall chimneys and tower. This group of five houses, Montebello, Smallcombe Grove, Fiesole, La Casetta and Casa Bianca is one of the most delightful enclaves in Bath, now bisected by the wide road which was then little more than a lane.

143 Shopfront at 1 Terrace Walk, 1750

144 Shopfronts in Queen Street. c.1750

Since the middle of the eighteenth century the appearance of the central city streets had changed as Bath became famous for its luxury shops. Window shopping became a favourite pastime for the city's fashionable visitors rather than a necessity for the permanent residents. The attractive shopfront was a new building type. Until the seventeenth-century European shops had scarcely changed from those in Imperial Rome. They were simply a room open to the street and divided from it only by a counter, and shutters at night. As in Rome, they were frequently built as a source of rent in prosperous houses where the occupants lived on the upper floors, and in Italy, though never in England, even occasionally in palaces of the nobility. Gilmore's 1694 map of Bath has a border consisting of engravings of the 36 most notable houses in the city (all but one of them now long lost). Five of them had shops of this type, including the mansions of Alderman Burns at Bear Corner and Alderman Chapman in Staul (Stall) Street. Two other substantial houses in Staul Street had them, and one in Abbey Churchyard. They were purely functional, there was nothing about them to encourage idlers to browse. That began in the late seventeenth century when the use of expensive glass began to make permanent shopfronts and attractive window displays possible. Even so they were very slow to take off. A 1736 engraving of Bishopsgate in London shows that its shops were still a mixture of open-fronted and glass-fronted premises. (The former remained in use for butchers, fishmongers and so on until the mid-nineteenth century.) In the 1760s and 70s another change took place. The practice of numbering houses in a street had not yet begun, so premises were known by their hanging signs – 'at the sign of the Golden Fleece' etc. – but in 1762, after many accidents caused by their falling, a London Building Act prohibited them in the capital. The Act had no force outside London, but fashion had almost equal power and most communities throughout the country quickly followed. This encouraged the evolution of fascia boards above the shopfront upon which the traders could identify themselves and their trades. In 1807 Southey wrote that in London all shops had them (although that must have been an exaggeration).

The earliest surviving shopfront in Bath is said to be at 1 Terrace Walk, in a house built (possibly by the elder John Wood) in 1750. (143) In fact it wasn't a shopfront in the strict sense of the word because it was originally a Coffee Rooms, and the windows were not intended for the display of goods but to reveal the enticing interior to passers-by. The four stone Ionic columns are convincingly 1750-ish, and so are the arches, semi-circular over each of the windows and elliptical over the wider doorway. The glazing bars are certainly modern, and the modillion cornice may be an early nineteenth-century modernisation. In Queen Street there is a small group of unaltered shopfronts of about the same date which, being too humble to have been modernised later, survive intact. (144) The narrow alley-like Queen Street, with its granite setts and Pennant slab pavements, still retains its mid-eighteenth-century character, only now missing the

145 Sally Lunn's 17th-century house with early 19th-century shopfront

hanging signs it must once have had. The shopfronts, without fascias, are simply shallow canted bay windows – shallow because the street and its pavements were too narrow to have allowed anything deeper. They were purely functional with scarcely any attempt to make them attractive, though their hanging signs must have occasionally been so. Signboards were painted by tradesmen house painters who had to be able to undertake an extraordinary range of tasks – grind pigments to make their own paints, letter, simulate wood graining and marble, cut and apply stencils, hang wallpaper, apply gold leaf and paint pub and shop signs. Some of them even painted the primitive portraits and views one occasionally sees in the salerooms. More sophisticated shops did sometimes employ artist painters, the most famous being the Parisian art dealer Gersaint's shop-sign painted by Watteau.[2]

2 Now in the Gemäldega-lerie, Berlin.

146 Shopfront at 2 Abbey Street, c.1800

148 Shopfronts at 114 and 116 Walcot Street, c.1800. Two shops now amalgamated into one

147 Shopfronts at 7 and 8 Old Bond Street, c.1800 or just after. Number 7 has lost its original glazing

A more pleasing variant of these flat-fronted bay windows were bow-fronts, Bath's most famous example being Sally Lunn's shop at 4 North Parade Passage. (145) Its glazing and cornice are original, and the fanlight over the modern door probably slightly later. Having no fascia the shop must have had a hanging sign. In the early nineteenth century bowed shop windows became extremely popular. Possibly the most charming of the many in Bath is the double-bowed 2 Abbey Street with its undulating fascia and beautifully curved guard-rails to one of the basement windows. (146) The most spectacular is the surviving pair of an original row of eight double bow-fronted shopfronts in Old Bond Street, of about 1800. The undulating entablature over both shops and the glazing of number 8 are original but number 7 has modern plate glass. (147) A more unusual variant is the pair of shops at 114 and 116 Walcot Street, (148) where the houses are flat fronted but the whole composition is given great charm by the shopfronts projecting forward from them in a gentle curve.

In those years a basic shop pattern developed which lasted throughout the century – a central shopfront with its glazed entrance door on one side and solid door on the other giving access to the house above. There are several handsome examples in Argyle Street, which became a fashionable shopping street in the late 1820s. The best is the shop which has been occupied by

149 Hale's shopfront of 1828 on the left, and the Boater pub of 1809 on the right

150 Shopfront of 1858 in a house of 1840, corner of John and Quiet Streets

Hale's the chemists since 1828. (149) Its front is entirely original and glorified by the Coade-stone coat of Queen Charlotte's arms which Mr Hale bought from Mrs Coade's catalogue and then had painted. A later, typically Victorian example of the two-door shop is on the corner of John and Quiet Streets and appears to be substantially unaltered since it was built in 1858 in a house built a couple of decades earlier. (150) By this time the Georgian glazing bar had almost had its day, particularly in shopfronts where the heavy plate glass required something more substantial to support it. Here, and in thousands of other shops throughout the country, the glass is held by slender wooden colonnettes, the cornice is supported by scrolls and the frieze has a row of decorative blocks. As the century progressed each of these features tended to become more elaborated.

9 The later nineteenth century and beyond

The 1840s were very prosperous years in the west of England and saw a great deal of new building. In 1840 Bath's City Architect G. P. Manners laid out a short new road connecting the north side of Queen Square to the Upper Bristol Road. It was an obvious convenience for traffic wanting to get into or out from the northern part of the city, but ultimately it was to have a devastating effect on Queen Square, making it the traffic hell it is today. The north side of Charlotte Street, as the new road was called, is important architecturally for two buildings at its east end, each of which introduced a new classical style to Bath. The first and better of the two was built in 1840 by a London architect, George Alexander, for the Bath Savings Bank. (151) As Henry-Russell Hitchcock pointed out in 1954, it was heavily influenced by Charles Barry's Reform Club in London's Pall Mall.[1] Indeed, it was started before Barry's Club was completed. The Club and the Bank introduced a new vocabulary into British classical architecture, the Italian High Renaissance forms of Sangallo's Palazzo Farnese in Rome which was completed by Michelangelo. The Palazzo's frontage consists of three rows of equally stressed windows crowned by Michelangelo's huge cornice. Apart from the small columns forming the aedicules framing the first- and second-floor windows, there are no other columns or pilasters, merely long and short coigns at each corner. For his Reform Club Barry repeated this pattern but instead of the alternating pediments on the first floor he used only triangular ones, and instead of Michelangelo's tall pedimented windows on the top floor, used the more usual nearly square windows. Alexander's bank was much shorter than the Reform Club, three bays instead of nine, under a very heavy cornice. His side elevations are also of three bays, so the building is a beautifully proportioned nearly cubic block. He sensibly reverted to Sangallo's pattern of alternating pediments, and introduced two dynamic features of his own – the setting-back of the top two storeys from the bottom one, and the extremely long quoins at the lower level. Later an inoffensive porch was added to the street front, but otherwise the façades remain as he designed them. According to Hitchcock, Alexander's forceful little design appealed to other bankers and had many imitators throughout the country, but this one didn't remain a bank for very long, becoming the home of the Holburne Museum until it moved to its present building in 1896. It now houses the city's Register Office.

In 1845, the Moravians, abandoning their tiny chapel in Monmouth Street, commissioned James Wilson whom we met in the last chapter, to build them a bigger one next door to the Savings Bank. (152) It was the first appearance in Bath of the baroque which was to remain one of the dominant classical styles throughout the rest of the century in Britain – not the tame and worn-out provincial baroque of the early eighteenth-century houses in the city, but the whole-hearted

1 Alexander was understandably fond of his miniature version of Barry's Reform Club. According to Hitchcock, in 1847 he built a very similar one for the Sheffield Athenaeum and Mechanics Institution.

151 Bath Savings Bank, now the Register Office. George Alexander, 1840

seventeenth-century baroque of Hawksmoor and Vanbrugh. The chapel's façade is dominated by a great vertical portico of Corinthian columns in antis. The Bank and the Chapel make fascinating neighbours, very different from each other but wonderfully compatible. Their main features are of very different scales and characters, but they both have an underlying power and force, and neither has any remaining vestige of Georgian character. George Alexander's Bank is one of the most impressive commercial buildings in the city. (Like the Bank, the Chapel is no longer used by its original owners, now being a Christian Science church.)

152 Moravian Chapel, now
the Christian Science
Church. James Wilson,
1845

Most nineteenth-century churches in Bath, as elsewhere, were Gothic, and not therefore within the scope of this book. None is of the very highest quality, but two deserve mention because they fit into the classical city so beneficially. One, designed in 1840-5 by James Wilson, the architect of the Moravian Chapel and the Walcot Schools, is St Stephen's, strategically positioned at the fork at the top of Lansdown Road, so that its tower closes the view and provides that part of the hillside with a much needed vertical. An even more strategically positioned church tower is St Michael with St Paul's, built in 1834-7 to the design of G.P. Manners, the City Architect. Its delightful tower, with its cascading mouldings taken from Salisbury Cathedral, is enormously important in the inner city townscape. The way it closes the view looking east along the south side of Queen Square and its continuation Wood Street is one of the area's most intense visual pleasures. (153) No classical building could have this impact, depending as it does on the extreme contrast between the tower's aggressive, spiky Gothic and its quietly classical surroundings. The tower pops up unexpectedly but always happily in several other views in the surrounding streets.

Like the Gothic churches, none of the city's nineteenth-century classical ones are of much architectural distinction, but one, which is outside the city in the west wing of Prior Park, is superlative but hidden away from the street and therefore little known. In the first half of the nineteenth century the English Roman Catholic Church, particularly in its western Vicarate, had architectural ambitions well beyond its financial means. Bishop Baines, having spent many years in Rome, had become his church's leading advocate of the classical style for churches, in opposition to Pugin's contemporary advocacy of Gothic. In 1829, the year of Parliament's emancipation of the Church from the restrictions previously imposed upon it, he bought Prior Park mansion and grounds to use as a seminary, and commissioned H.E. Goodridge to design a huge domed church to stand behind, and tower above it. Then, anticipating the time when the English Church would be authorised by Rome to re-introduce diocesan organisation, he started work on a huge Pro Cathedral in Bristol. The Bath church was never started: of the Bristol cathedral only the forlorn trunks of huge unfinished Doric columns remain to mock his dreams. He died in 1843 and in 1844 his successor commissioned Joseph John Scoles (1798-1863), the leading Catholic church architect of his time, to demolish Prior Park's west wing and build the church of St Paul on its site.

When it was half-built work stopped when the church had to face financial reality and sell Prior Park. For 30 years the church remained unfinished and roofless until the Bishop of the newly created Diocese of Clifton bought back the house to use as the boys' school which it remains to this day, now with girls as well. Scoles having died nineteen years earlier, the Bishop employed his ordained architect son to complete the

153 Baldwin's house at the bottom of Milsom Street and the spire of St Michael's with St Paul's closing the view along Wood Street

church. It was finally consecrated in 1882 and work stopped, though the decorative part of the exterior is far from complete and internally some of the Corinthian capitals at the west end remain as un-carved blocks.

The unfinished exterior of the church finally destroyed the already damaged symmetry of Wood's two wings. The interior is superb, the few bits of uncompleted carving of little significance. (154) Neil Jackson has pointed to a probable French inspiration, Chalgrin's St Philippe du Roule in Paris of 1768, though there are several French church interiors of this general type which Scoles will have seen in his youthful four years travelling on the Continent and in the Levant. Chalgrin's Ionic church has wider aisles, giving its interior a more airy character, and it has only painted coffering on its tunnel vault. The interior of Scoles's Corinthian

154 Prior Park, church of
St Paul. J.J. Scoles,
1844-82

church is more tightly compressed, its genuinely coffered vault is more powerfully insistent, and the two closely spaced ranks of Corinthian columns focus attention on the altar. There is nothing quite like this beautiful, dynamic interior, in France or anywhere else.

Most buildings display the characteristics of their time, so that those from a period we enjoy have features which we have learnt to love and upon which we focus. Our enjoyment of these can sometimes hide the fact that they have other features which are discordant, or make it intrusive in its location. To the uncritical observer it seems that the eighteenth century, for example, was a Golden Age when architects could do no wrong. In fact, of course, there have been ugly and damagingly intrusive buildings in all periods. Earlier in this book we have seen Eveleigh's ugly Grosvenor development and John Pinch's intrusive three houses on the west side of Queen Square. The National Westminster Bank at the top of Milsom Street (now a fish restaurant) has all the rollicking gusto that we so much enjoy in Victorian commercial buildings, but it disguises the fact that it has ludicrous faults. It was built in 1865 to the design of William Willcox (c.1838-1923). (155) The bottom three storeys are a version of the conventional Italian pattern of a rusticated base supporting giant two-storey Corinthian columns. Unfortunately the site was too narrow to accommodate the type of façade Willcox wanted to build. As a result the windows are too tightly

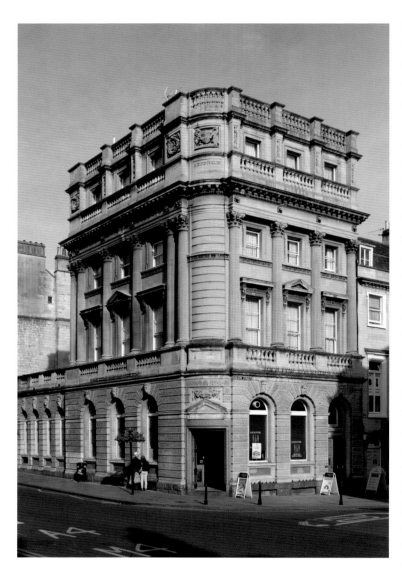

155 Bank at the top of Milsom Street. William Willcox, 1865. Top floor added by Willcox in 1884

crammed between the columns. This is exacerbated by his treatment of the corner, which he rounded into a tall quadrant, a device much used at that time by the lowly-regarded designers of London pubs. They plastered their quadrants and painted them with the names of the pubs in exotic lettering. Such cockney flamboyance was out of place on a bank, especially one in Bath, but then why further cramp the two façades by having the quadrant? Nineteen years later, in 1884, Willcox was commissioned to add an attic storey. It was this that made a foolish building into a positively nasty one, the top storey looking what it was, an afterthought, and looking what it wasn't, an addition by a later architect out of sympathy with his predecessor's work below. Plenty of architects, before and since, have had to add one or more storeys to an existing building, but it would be hard to find an example as inept as this, especially one where the addition was designed by the original architect. It makes the building top-heavy, and by the strengthening of the original cornice and balustrade somehow makes it look like three

156 Grand Pump Room
Hotel. Wilson and
Willcox, 1865,
demolished 1959.
Image from *Bath in
Time*

buildings, heaped one on top of the other. Whilst the bank was under construction Willcox joined with James Wilson (architect of the splendid Moravian Chapel) to form Wilson and Willcox, a partnership which was responsible for several Gothic churches in Bath and elsewhere, some of them very enjoyable. It is clear that the partnership was capable of producing fine buildings. Possibly Willcox was the business rather than the design partner, a not uncommon arrangement in those years. By the time the attic was added in 1884 the partnership had been enlarged to become Wilson, Willcox and Wilson.

In 1865, the year Wilson and Willcox was formed, the partners entered an architectural competition to design the huge Grand Pump Room Hotel in Stall Street, opposite the Pump Room. The competition was won by the City Architect Major Charles Edward Davis (1862-1902) who was awarded the first premium of £200, but there was some sort of dispute and the commission was given to Wilson and Willcox who had been awarded the second premium of £100. Their design was much influenced by the New Louvre in Paris, the design of which was then very fashionable in England, but the modified design they built was less highly elaborated and a great deal cheaper. (156) On plan it consisted of a wide forecourt flanked by wings. The elevation was an elongated version of their Milsom Street bank's front – a rusticated arcade at ground level, supporting a two-storey colonnade of eight giant Corinthian columns, a very deep entablature and attic. Apart from slightly simplified windows they could almost have used the same detail drawings. The wings, however, had very simplified versions of the New Louvre's

high-domed roofs. I can remember when I was a student being thrilled by the hotel before it was demolished in 1959, and can testify that this mix of sixteenth-century Palladian and grand nineteenth-century French baroque did not look as bizarre as it sounds. A further attraction was the fact that the wide forecourt faced onto Abbey Churchyard, combining with it to make a very large open space across Stall Street. The hotel must have suffered commercially after the Empire Hotel opened in 1902 with more up-to-date facilities and enjoying wider and more attractive views. After being requisitioned by the Admiralty throughout the 1939-45 war, the Grand Pump Room Hotel never recovered, and its value becoming less than that of its site, demolition became inevitable. Although far from being in the architectural first rank, it was a regrettable loss which would not be tolerated today. I, though few others, mourned its passing.

In 1865 Davis built the little police station in Orange Grove. (157) Now a restaurant, it is rather dwarfed by nearby larger subsequent buildings with strong personalities so it is easily overlooked, but it amply repays examination. It is a tiny version of a sixteenth-century Italian palazzo. Its ground floor is heavily rusticated and its severely plain first floor is divided into

158 Jolly's shopfront.
C.E. Davis, 1879

three bays, the central one slightly recessed, and all three containing an arched window. The bays are linked together by their cornices which continue as a moulding running round the building. The structure is capped by a widely projecting bracketed cornice. It remained a police station for 101 years, until the new, larger and infinitely duller replacement was built in Manvers Street. Davis, like most architects at that time, could work in almost any style, but showed a particular liking and understanding of Italian sixteenth-century architecture. The nephew of Edward Davis, he was extremely prolific, with buildings large and small all over Bath. His little Shakespeare Memorial, which is a simple Roman altar in his uncle's Royal Victoria Park, is one of many tiny works with which, as City Architect, he enriched the city. Nearby is another, the Park's bandstand. Not much larger is one of his several privately commissioned buildings, the ornate shopfront for Jolly's store in Milsom Street of 1879. (158) His largest building was his worst, the lumpen Arts and Crafts Jacobethan Empire Hotel of 1902 (now flats) which is simply an enormous heap of ill-related architectural motifs. His greatest gift to his native city was his discovery and excavation of the Roman Baths.

159 Green Park Station
     booking hall, waiting
     rooms and office.
     J.H. Sanders, 1868-9

160 The train shed. J.C.
     Crossley engineer,
     1868-9

The City Council's efforts at this time to rejuvenate the Baths and to increase the numbers of visitors, decided the Midland Railway Company to run a branch into the city from their Bristol to Birmingham line. They managed to achieve what the Great Western had not, a station located almost in the heart of the city. As it was only a few hundred yards from Queen Square that was the name they gave it. When the Company was nationalised in 1948 it was renamed Green Park Station, but only 16 years later both line and station were closed. When the unappealing Great Western Station was built in the 1840s it was not surprising that it should be Gothic, then at the height of its national popularity. In 1860s Bath, when Gothic was rarely used for anything other than churches and chapels, the city's eighteenth-century architecture was beginning to be admired again, so the choice of a classical style for the new Queen Square station was almost inevitable. The block containing the booking hall, waiting rooms etc at the front of the station (159) was designed by the Company's architect J. H. Sanders, and the surprisingly large train shed behind by its Chief Engineer J. C. Crossley. (160) Although they are attached, architecturally and structurally they are separate buildings, both of them splendid. The width of the beautifully proportioned Bath-stone frontage block was dictated by the width of the train shed, and the height by the need for only two storeys. This produced a relatively long low façade which Sanders heightened by putting a balustrade on the roof. He treated the façade as a wide centrepiece with narrow side wings. The ground floor is rusticated in the Victorian Baroque manner, with the horizontal stone joints emphasised but the vertical ones not. At first-floor level the centrepiece is an Ionic colonnade, the columns being widely spaced to frame windows and their surrounds. Each of the wings has the familiar Bath pedimented tripartite window which is to be seen in several places in the city, such as on the Carved House in Gay Street and in Bathwick Street. The result is a delight, an under-rated façade paying its respects to its historic context but not copying slavishly. (It would be greatly improved if the iron and glass canopy attached to it could be removed.) Sanders was a much more subtle designer than most of the architects who worked for the railway companies. By the 1860s glass-roofed iron-vaulted train sheds with their huge spans were no longer a novelty, but were still much admired as daring technology. J.C. Crossley's Bath roof, naturally enough, is reminiscent of the company's St Pancras Station. It consists of slender segmental arched iron ribs supporting iron purlins which in turn support the glass. The station's frontage block is now a restaurant and the train shed a Sainsbury's car park.

Until the middle of the nineteenth century ratepayers in Britain had kept the work of local authorities to a minimum, opposing educational, public health and other urgently needed reforms in order to keep the rates low (for an example see the footnote on pages 96-97). By the last few decades of the century the public conscience had been awakened and the role of local government was transformed by being given, or by voluntarily taking on, a large number of new responsibilities. Most old town halls were inadequate to accommodate the greatly increased staff needed to deal with them, so a large number of new town halls were built and old ones extended. In these last decades of Britain's unchallenged power and wealth the country could afford to do this magnificently. At the same time there was a growing belief that there

161 The Guildhall.
The southern wing of
John McKean Brydon's
1893-7 extension on
the right, with the five
bays of Baldwin's 1788
building on the left

should be a specifically English style of architecture as there had been in the past. The Arts and Crafts style met this very well for domestic and other small buildings, but was hardly suitable for town halls, or, as we have seen, for the huge Empire Hotel. Fortunately there was a growing enthusiasm for the work of the indisputably English Christopher Wren, whose churches and palaces were considered to be suitable models for large public buildings.

Baldwin's Guildhall had become as inadequate as any of the British town halls, so the City Council took expert opinion and was advised that as a fine eighteenth-century building it should be retained but given a large extension. The City Architect might have expected to be given the job of designing it, but it was decided to hold a competition from which he was excluded because he was under a cloud at that time, a workman having been killed in the partial collapse of the Old Bath which he was rebuilding. The competition was won by a Scottish architect called John McKean Brydon (1840-1901) whose Chelsea Town Hall was much admired at that time. He was a member of the Art Workers' Guild which had recently been founded to bring back the close association of architecture, sculpture and painting which had been lost at the end of the medieval period, and was one of the leaders of the demand for an English style of architecture based on the work of Wren and his great contemporaries. In a talk given to the Architectural Association in 1889 he said the Wren style was 'in some way superior to even the

162 Brydon's Guildhall
extension.
Frieze on the corner
carved by G.A. Lewson

Italian Renaissance.' It was 'a precious heritage' the study of which could 'bring forth fruits worthy of the high ideal'. His winning design proposed a long symmetrical façade of which the old Guildhall was the centrepiece, with new wings turning at one end into the Orange Grove and at the other into Bridge Street. (161)

Baldwin had designed his Guildhall façade as a cubic block tied down to the ground by low single-storey screen walls to enclose the market behind. (92) Much later the screens were replaced by heavier structures which were not sympathetic to Baldwin's more delicate design. They in turn were demolished by Brydon who needed the space for his extensions. He took advantage of the fact that the Guildhall was built nearly midway between the Orange Grove and Bridge Street corners, so he could use it as his centre-piece, though he had to slightly shorten his southern wing by spacing his windows a little more narrowly; an adjustment so discreet that very few people ever notice it. The centrepieces of his wings thus occur at the two street corners and are therefore curved. They are a paraphrase of Baldwin's centrepiece, and articulated by tower-like projecting features which are versions of the façade on either side of Baldwin's centrepiece. The mechanics of the paraphrase are fascinating. Unlike Baldwin's centre his is recessed and its flanking walls project. Like Baldwin's his ground floor is rusticated and the two storeys above are not, and his centre has giant Corinthian columns, but more widely spaced. Between the first and second floors he has a deep sculptured frieze. (162) This is an early example of the influence of Belcher and Pite's Institute of Chartered Accountants building in Moorgate which beautifully exemplified the ideals of the Art Workers' Guild, and was receiving huge coverage in the architectural press at that time. It has to be said that Hamo Thorneycroft's

163 One of Brydon's cupolas

glorious frieze on the London building looks more at ease there than G. A. Lewson's in Bath because Belcher's building has very deeply cut rustication and other Mannerist devices (then called Baroque) which suit it, whilst Bryden's is still in Baldwin's much simpler Adamish style where the huge frieze looks over-emphatic. At each end of the long façade facing onto the High Street, Brydon crowned each of his tower-like features with a large Mannerist/Baroque cupola, using another of Belcher's Mannerist devices, heavily blocked columns. (163) His southern wing housed Council offices, his northern wing a Technical School (now more Council offices).

Then, in 1893, Brydon was given another commission, to build a screen wall to enclose a small courtyard between the south end of his Guilhall extension and Charles Davis's Police Station. (157) Based on motifs taken from Sebastiano Serlio's *Regole Generali*, it is the most purely Mannerist of all the incidents on this enormously long line of buildings. Brydon developed Serlio's motifs with great imagination. His screen is loosely based on the Roman Triumphal Arch pattern, with a large central arch flanked by smaller pedestrian flat arches. The large central arch is supported by heavily blocked Doric columns, and the side openings have circular port holes above them – a motif of which Serlio was particularly fond, but treated here in a much more decorative way than the simple openings in the Italian master's designs. The composition is topped by a heavy balustrade.

164 Victoria Art Gallery. J.M. Brydon, 1897-1900

Whilst the screen was under construction Brydon was given a further commission, this time to design the Victoria Art Gallery which extends his line of buildings along Bridge Street up to its corner with Grand Parade. The Gallery was not the result of a responsibility newly imposed on Councils by the government, but was prompted by the civic pride which was such a notable feature of that period. The immediate spur to action was a desire to commemorate the Queen's Diamond Jubilee. (164) Brydon continued the lines of the adjoining Technical School, but substituted Ionic for the Corinthian which he had taken over from Baldwin's building. He placed the entrance on the corner facing Pulteney Bridge, with a dome over the vestibule. A subsidiary entrance was needed for the Reference Library, which Brydon placed in the centre

165 J.M. Brydon's building
to house the Roman
Baths, 1894

of the Bridge Street façade, with a statue of the Queen in a niche over it. The four smaller niches on either side are blank. Internally, the first-floor art gallery is, as usual, coved and top-lit, and dignified by a cast of that ultimate symbol of High Art, the Parthenon frieze, running round it (which was given to the city by Brydon).

The rather commonplace dome which Brydon added to Baldwin's building is badly out of character with its eighteenth-century delicacy, but the most serious criticism of his extensions is that they reduce the original building, which was designed to stand alone and be seen in the round, into just a façade in a long line of façades. That was implicit in the programme which Brydon had been given and he can't be blamed for it. He made the Guildhall the centrepiece of his design, and he designed everything to play up to it: he could have done no more.

All that was not Brydon's only work in Bath. In 1894 he won a competition to design a building to house the Roman Baths which had been discovered a few years earlier. His winning entry was considered to be too expensive, but he was given the commission for the variant which we can enjoy today. (165) It consists of a splendid baroque domed concert room with a baroque-ish Palladian front facing onto Abbey Churchyard. Although a respectful neighbour to the Baldwin/Palmer botch-up beside it, it is a far better façade. He linked the two with a single-storey wing which he repeated symmetrically on the other side as a screen wall which then turns the corner to wrap around the Roman Bath. This building and the great composition of the Guildhall and its extensions, the screen wall and the Art Gallery were Brydon's finest work, and a magnificent contribution to Bath's long history of fine classical buildings.[2]

So Bath's nineteenth-century architecture ended with a bang. The city's history in the first half of the twentieth century was a long drawn-out whimper: the population remained almost static; industry slept; the Georgian terraces decayed and their houses were divided into flats. One superb little Roman Catholic church was built, Byzantine, not classical, the great Sir Giles Gilbert Scott's church of Our Lady and St Alphege, designed in 1927. A few classical buildings were erected but they were no longer the work of particularly gifted architects. The best was the splendid Post Office in New Bond Street of 1923, designed by somebody in H.M. Office of Works. (166)

The second half of the century was much more dynamic, but initially more notable for the demolition of modest Georgian terraces than the erection of anything interesting. However, the huge programme of repair, restoration and façade cleaning described in Chapter 1 transformed the appearance of the city. In the areas of Bath away from the Georgian terraces it was accepted that new buildings could be in a contemporary style, though they were required to be faced with Bath stone, or occasionally, as in the case of Farrell Grimshaw's fine factory for Herman Miller of 1975, with stone-coloured panels. By the end of the century it was becoming accepted that even in the city centre it was absurd to dress every new building in eighteenth-century clothes. The most notable example of this was Nicholas Grimshaw's brilliant New Royal Bath of 1999-2003.

One site proved to be extremely controversial, an old quarry set back from the top of Lansdown Road. It had once housed the demolished Cavendish Lodge but been neglected and increasingly scruffy for twenty years. It was situated below Cavendish and Lansdown Crescents, so it could scarcely have been more sensitive. The City Council had given the site outline planning permission for housing, but presumably regretting having done so had refused nine successive applications as being unsuitable. In 1986 William Bertram was commissioned to draw up designs and make a tenth application. He is an extremely gifted Bath architect whose buildings have usually been designed in historic styles. He was then working for the Prince of Wales at Highgrove and was later to design Winston Churchill's tomb in the churchyard at Bladon just outside the park at Blenheim. At the back of the quarry he designed a block of twenty flats in the form of a large Palladian house approached from Cavendish Road by a formal drive flanked by two lodges. (167) The application was refused, his client appealed successfully,[3] but a group of conservationists referred the decision to judicial review, and when that failed, to the House

2 It was contemporary with his largest work, the colossal Government offices on the corner of Parliament Square, London, which alas were cruelly altered during construction after his death in 1901.

3 I must declare an interest. Bertram's solicitor asked me to act as his Expert Witness at the Inquiry. After examining the design drawings and recognising their quality, I accepted the commission with some enthusiasm.

of Lords, again unsuccessfully. The opposition appeared to have been mainly a desire to keep the site undeveloped, but at the Public Inquiry and frequently since, the use of Bath stone un-pointed rubble walling as a facing for parts of the three buildings was criticised as being foreign to Bath. It is true that the city's eighteenth- and nineteenth-century architects never used walling of this type on their buildings, but as we have seen throughout this book, each previous generation had introduced new motifs which then became accepted and traditional. Today nobody criticises John Wood because he introduced Palladianism to Bath, or Thomas Gandy for introducing Greek architecture, Edward Davis for introducing Italianate architecture, or J. M. Brydon for introducing Mannerism. For two and a half thousand years classical architecture has never stood still but constantly developed. William Bertram gave it another push. People wishing to denigrate his new Cavendish Lodge say it is a pastiche, a copy. It is a remarkable confusion of mind to criticise it for being a copy and at the same time condemn it for not being one.

In 2011 the long-awaited extension at the back of the Holburne Museum was opened. The winning entry in the competition for its design was by the London architect Eric Parry. It evoked cries of rage from the blinkered, who did everything they could to stop it being built. Closely ringed by trees, the building is invisible from Great Pulteney Street or anywhere else in the city. In this verdant setting its cladding of lustrous slabs of green ceramic separated by irregularly spaced vertical ceramic fins, some of which hang down below the others, give it something of the appearance of falling water or a cascade of foliage. The effect is mesmerising, changing as the light changes, sparkling in sunlight and going a subdued grey-green in shade.

Architectural style alone should never be a factor in deciding whether a proposed new building is acceptable or not. It never has been in the past: Brydon's Mannerist and Baroque extensions to the Guildhall and Manners's Gothic St Michael's in Broad Street greatly enriched the city. What matters is quality, and above all, respect for context. New Cavendish Lodge nestles

167 Cavendish Lodge. William Bertram, 1986-96. Lansdown Crescent is in the distance above

beautifully into its little niche on Lansdown Hill, the New Royal Bath squeezes companionably into its tightly congested city site, and the Holburne extension sits among its trees as though it has always been there.

In 2010 the much disliked and cheaply built Southgate shopping centre was replaced by a modestly pleasant layout of pedestrian streets and squares, paying their respects to Georgian Bath with a few classical details, but with nothing of the real thing's guts and force, and without any of the comforts of the more recent covered shopping malls in Britain.

So in the decades on either side of 2000 Bath acquired three buildings of notably high quality, New Cavendish Lodge, the New Royal Bath and the Holburne extension, and a shopping centre of unremarkable quality. All three of the architecturally outstanding buildings have been venomously attacked, the mediocre one has been received in relative peace. The lesson which this puts before intending builders in Bath is obvious, and unless public perceptions change, the implications for the city's future architectural health are ominous.

Glossary of terms used in this book

Numerals in brackets refer to caption numbers for the photographs in which the described feature appears.

Antefix: the ornament on the eaves of Greek temples covering the ends of the tiles, but used by the Greek Revivalists simply as roof ornaments. **(112)**

Antis: **antae**: pilasters on a wall responding to columns built in line with them. The columns are then said to be in antis. **(112, 115)**

Apron: a raised stone or brick panel below a window. **(9)**

Arcade: a row of arches supported by columns or piers. **(14)**

Ashlar: walling where the faces of the stones are dressed smooth. In good work the joints are extremely thin, requiring very accurate stone cutting. Much of the ashlar masonry in Bath is of superlative quality.

Attached or engaged columns: columns appearing to be partially sunk into a wall. The degree to which they are free from the wall determines their name – half or three-quarter columns. **(106)**

Attic: a storey above the cornice with its external wall continuing the wall surface below. A storey built into the roof and lit by dormers is a garret. **(10)**

Baroque: European art of the seventeeth century and a little later. In English architecture the style was governed by a considerable amount of classical restraint.

Bolection: a heavy S-shaped convex moulding. When used as window, door or fireplace surrounds they usually project beyond the surface of the wall. **(8)**

Capital: the feature at the top of a column, pilaster or pier.

Cill band: a band of stone continuing the line of the window cills. **(3)**

Classical: a word which has gathered too many meanings. Strictly it applies to the world of ancient Greece and Rome, more loosely to buildings and other artefacts using Greek or Roman elements, e.g. columns, entablatures, pediments etc. From this the meaning has been extended to works of art governed by the spirit of classical art, but not using its elements. (The popular use of the word is often ridiculous: much 'classical' music, for instance, is not in the least classical.)

Corinthian order: slender fluted columns with capitals of stylised acanthus leaves. **(156)**

Cornice: the projecting, shadow-creating, top element of an entablature.

Cove: a large, sometimes huge, concave moulding, usually making the junction between wall and ceiling. **(95)**

Doric order: stubby columns, usually fluted and usually supporting an entablature with triglyths and metopes in the frieze. Greek Doric columns never had bases but architects until the Greek Revival most often gave them one. **(34)**

Echinus: the moulding of a Doric capital. Always subtly convex in Greek buildings but concave in Bath's Doric House. **(112)**.

Elevation: the face of a building or an internal wall: more strictly a scale drawing of it.

Entablature: the series of mouldings supported by classical columns or doorways, windows etc. An entablature consists of an architrave, a frieze and, at the top, a cornice. **(34, 112)**

Frieze: the middle member of an entablature. Occasionally it can be very large and sculptural, as at the corners of Bath's Guildhall extension. **(93, 164)**

Giant columns: columns which extend through two or more storeys. Tall columns which don't do this are not called giant. **(15)**

Gibbs Surround: the surround of a window or door, consisting of long and short quoins at the sides and heavy voussoirs at the top. **(30)**

Hexastyle: six-columned. **(15)**

Ionic order: slender columns, usually fluted, with capitals consisting of volutes. The spirals of a volute are extremely difficult to draw and carve. The better Georgian masons were admirably adept at this. **(107)**

Lunette: a semi-circular window or other opening.

Mannerism: in Italy the style of the last three-quarters of the sixteenth century, which developed, and in architecture sometimes perverted, previously accepted norms. Influential in sixteenth- and seventeenth-century England through the often bizarre and grotesque engravings in pattern books, most of them from the Low Countries.

Metope: the square or rectangular space between the triglyths in a Doric entablature. They can be either plain or carved with ornaments. Palladio advised that when such ornaments were used they should be simple in shape and only a few motifs be used. John Wood ignored this in his Circus and was much criticised for it. Today most critics would probably consider that the result fully justified his deviation from authority. **(34)**

Modillion cornice: one supported on brackets, regularly spaced so that a bracket is always positioned over each column, window and door. In practice this means that the precise positioning of such features is determined by the spacing of the modillions. A similar rule applies to triglyths. **(41)**

Mullion: a vertical stone or wooden support dividing a

window into separate lights.

Orders: classical architecture was based on the five orders – Doric, Ionic, Corinthian, Tuscan and Composite, only the first three being used in the buildings described in this book. Each order had its own columns, entablatures and proportions, going down to the tiniest mouldings. Vitruvius described only four orders, the Composite probably not having been developed in his time. An invariable rule, as definitively illustrated by the Colosseum in Rome, is that in a multi-storey building the strongest-looking order, the sturdy Doric, should be used at the bottom, followed by the others in their degrees of slimness, Ionic, Corinthian and then Composite. (Tuscan was not used in multi-storey buildings.) Even in astylar classical buildings (those without columns etc.) the rules of proportioning apply.

Pavilion: (in classical buildings): the parts of a long façade which project forward symmetrically, usually at the centre and ends. **(15)**

Pediment: the triangular feature crowning a classical portico, window or door etc. Its bottom member is the cornice of the entablature below. **(15, 28)**

Picturesque: originally a scene reminiscent of a painting by Claude or Salvator Rosa etc; and then by extension, an important aesthetic movement extolling the wild, rugged and 'terrible'. The movement originated in England, the only important European art movement to do so, but soon, especially in landscape gardening, conquered Europe and America.

Pier: a heavy masonry support, as distinct from a slimmer column.

Pilaster: a flat column appearing to be partially sunk into a wall. **(113, 114)**

Quoins: large squared stones with V-cut emphasised joints, used to strengthen, actually or visually, the corners of buildings. They are sometimes all of the same length, sometimes alternately long and short. **(153, 154)**

Rococo: the last phase of the baroque. In Britain frequently used in interior decoration and furnishing, but rarely used externally.

Romanticism, romantic: Europe-wide art and literary movement of the decades on either side of 1800. The Picturesque was one of its most important aspects.

Rubble stonework: walls of stones left rough and uncut as delivered form the quarry. **(167)**

Rustication: facing masonry cut in large blocks with emphasised joints. There were numerous types. When used in Britain it was employed to give an appearance of solidity and strength to the lowest storey of a building. **(84)**

String course, or platband: a projecting stone band on the face of a wall. **(40)**

Stylobate: the base supporting a colonnade. **(112)**

Tabernacle: a term for a window surround consisting of attached columns supporting an entablature and usually a pediment. **(153)**

Tetrastyle: four-columned. **(29)**

Transom: a horizontal stone or wooden member dividing, with the mullions, a window into separate lights.

Triglyth: the vertically grooved blocks between the metopes of a Doric entablature. They should properly have two grooves and a half groove on each side, but architects and masons occasionally gave them more, probably through ignorance. When used (occasionally they and metopes were omitted) the triglyths and metopes must be spaced evenly across the whole façade, and a triglyth centred over each column or window. **(34)**

Vermiculation: a method of giving a heavy texture to stone blocks by carving their surface with irregular grooves reminiscent of worm tracks.

Vitruvius: an architect living in the reign of Augustus who wrote the only complete architectural treatise to come down to us from antiquity. His *De Architectura* in ten books (which we would call the ten sections of a book) was therefore treated with the utmost reverence by the architects of the Renaissance and later. His book preserves an enormous amount of traditional building, surveying and architectural knowledge from the Greek and Roman periods up to the first century AD, ranging from such matters as the making of bricks and the valuation of party walls, to the detailed design of each of the orders. Unfortunately none of the many manuscripts to survive are illustrated, and this, combined with his clumsy writing style, makes some of his work very obscure. This allowed subsequent architects to interpret it as they wished. The work, in its original Latin, was first printed in Italy in c.1487 and thereafter translated into most European languages, including English in 1692.

Voussoir: the splayed stones or bricks making a flat or curved arch. Their strength derives from the weight above being converted by their shape into horizontal forces which have to be resisted by sufficient walling on each side, or by some other force such as that from another arch. **(26)**

Additional reading

Not many British cities can have had as many books written about them, or their architecture, as Bath. Nobody could claim to have read them all, and only one or two librarians can even have heard of them all. The following is a brief appraisal of the most notable. Several contain full bibliographies, making superfluous the inclusion of one here.

Any list must begin with the great John Wood's *An Essay Towards a Description of the City of Bath*, published in 1742. There were several revised editions, the one of 1765 retitled less modestly *A description of Bath*, of which a facsimile was published in 1969. The book contains an enormous amount of valuable information, particularly about Wood's own buildings in Bath of which there are several engravings. The index is appalling and finding information is difficult and time consuming. Because it has been fully mined by the author of the present book, as well as by those listed below, only bibliophiles need to own a copy.

The first important book on Bath's architectural history was Mowbray Aston Green's *The Eighteenth Century Architecture of Bath* which was published in 1904 when he was a young architect in Bath. His was the foundation upon which all subsequent books were built. His excellent photographs are invaluable, showing buildings now lost and others still with us as they were then after a century's neglect, and before the twentieth century's further neglect and then restoration. His opinions are always interesting and often illuminating. The only disappointment is that, unlike most architects of his time, he was a poor draughtsman and his drawings, though valuable, are not a pleasure to look at. Copies are now rare and expensive but there has been a recent paperback edition. Any shelf of books on Bath and its architectural history should contain a copy.

The next history to appear was Walter Ison's magisterial *The Georgian Buildings of Bath* which was published 44 years later in 1948. It stands head and shoulders above all the others. Ison (1908-97) was also an architect and quite remarkably industrious, searching through the Bath archives and newspapers to accumulate an extraordinary body of information to which I and other subsequent writers have added only morsels. He was a fine draughtsman and his numerous plans and elevations in the book are immensely valuable. Like Mowbray Green before him, his opinions are always interesting, but expressed in a somewhat characterless prose. He and Green had an advantage that authors today do not. In their time owners welcomed people to see inside their houses. Because of the danger of burglary owners today are rarely welcoming. His

photographs show Bath's buildings as they were just after the war, damaged by bombs and years of neglect. They are themselves of historic value.

As their titles state, both Mowbray Green's and Ison's books stopped short of Victoria's reign, which in their time was considered to be an architectural wilderness. Nikolaus Pevsner's 1958 *Bristol and North Somerset* was the first to venture into this territory. His researchers relied heavily on Ison for the Georgian period, and added a little information on Bath's Victorian architecture, but the Professor's own opinions are often questionable. The book is now superseded by Andrew Foyle's replacement *Somerset: north and Bristol*.

The most important book on Bath's architectural history to appear in the second half of the twentieth century was Timothy Mowl and Brian Earnshaw's monograph *John Wood: Architect of Obsession* of 1988. Until their researches very little was known about Wood, and unless a cache of previously unknown documents is discovered, their book is unlikely to be superceded. As with all Prof. Mowl's books it is highly readable. It is time for a new edition.

Neil Jackson's *Nineteenth Century Bath: Architects and Architecture* of 1991 is the only book so far on the subject, though one can safely prophecise that there will be more. Pleasantly written but rather poorly illustrated, it contains useful information.

A truly remarkable guide book to Bath's buildings is Michael Forsyth's 2003 *Bath*, one of the most outstanding volumes in the outstanding Pevsner Architectural Guides series. It is a literary Tardis, containing an enormous amount of information in a volume 21.5cm x 12cm. Two copies are essential, one for the study and one for the car.

Prof. R. S. Neale's *Bath: a Social History 1680-1850* is much more than a valuable social history. It contains a great deal of economic history as well.

Prof. Barry Cunliffe's *Roman Bath* of 1995 is the most convenient book on his excavations.

Bath History, a series of paperback yearbooks published by Millstream Books, is invaluable. Each book contains 8 or so articles on various aspects of Bath's history, only some of which are architectural, but all of them interesting and some absorbing. A notable article, in volume 5 of 1994, is Jane Root's fully researched account of Thomas Baldwin's downfall.

Index